IT'S LIKE THAT

IT'S LIKE THAT

A SPIRITUAL MEMOIR

JOSEPH "REVEREND RUN" SIMMONS

WITH CURTIS L. TAYLOR

ST. MARTIN'S PRESS NEW YORK

www.stmartins.com

All photos by Ricky Powell

Design by Kathryn Parise

LIBRARY OF CONGRESS CATALOGING-IN-PUBLICATION DATA
Simmons, Joseph.
    It's like that : a spiritual memoir / Joseph "Reverend Run" Simmons
with Curtis L. Taylor.—1st. ed.
        p. cm.
    ISBN 0-312-20467-1
    1. Simmons, Joseph. 2. Run-D.M.C. (Musical group) 3. Rap
musicians—United States—Biography. 4. Clergy—United States—
Biography. 5. Christian biography—United States. I. Taylor, Curtis L.
II. Title.
BR1725.S4675 A3 2000
277.3'0825'092—dc21
    [B]   00-029685

First Edition: August 2000

10   9   8   7   6   5   4   3   2   1

To my Lord and Savior, Jesus Christ

Contents

Acknowledgments   ix

Foreword   xi

Introduction   1

1 Walk This Way   3

2 Run's House   9

3 The Son of Kurtis Blow   18

4 Raising Hell . . .   29

5 Spiritual Hard Times . . .   39

6 Wake Up   55

7 Down with the King   72

8 Giving: A Formula for Spiritual Success   85

9 The Birth of Reverend Run   104

10 Live an Enthusiastic Life   117

11 Love and Be Loved   127

12 Create a Wealth Mentality   138

13 My Crown Is Royal: Be a Pioneer   147

Acknowledgments

THERE ARE A NUMBER OF wonderful people who contributed in countless ways to making this book a reality, and at the risk of leaving some people out, I would like to thank a few special ones.

My wife, Justine, whom I love dearly. Without your support, none of this would have been possible.

My children, Vanessa, Angela, Jojo, Daniel, and Russell.

My father, Daniel Simmons, who has always been there.

My mother, Evelyn Simmons; may she rest in peace.

My brothers, Russell and Daniel Jr.

Jam Master Jay and D.M.C.

Bishop Jordan and Zoe Ministries.

My literary agents, Imar Hutchins and Dawn Marie Daniels, of Simply Said. Thanks for believing in the project and introducing me to the St. Martin's Press family. Thanks for showing the commitment, compassion, and tenacity to get the job done.

Thank you to everyone at St. Martin's Press, especially Sally Richardson. You've all treated me and my work with great respect and integrity.

A special thanks to Greg Cohn, who believed in me and fought hard to make the project happen from the beginning. Your special talents were appreciated; Dana Albarella and Josh Kendall, who took over for Greg and showed just as much enthusiasm and talent shepherding the book through its final stages; Bob Wallace for his vision and understanding that hip-hop is not just music, and for knowing that books like this can be successful; my appreciation to everyone in marketing; and to art director Henry Yee, for going above and beyond the call of duty to design a beautiful jacket—he worked tirelessly for the right photographs and cover layout. And to Eric Blamoville, Charlie Steler, Kathy, Ray, Smith, Perry and Chris, and Curtis L. Taylor, who helped me pull this together.

Finally, a special thanks to all of the wonderful fans who have supported Run-D.M.C. through the years. You have made me the King of Rap.

—Peace, Reverend Run

Curtis L. Taylor wishes to thank God for all His many blessings; Imar Hutchins and Dawn Marie Daniels for their guidance, support, and friendship; Chandra Sparks for her time, encouragement, and creative input.

To Reverend Run for the opportunity and sharing your gifts with the world (you are special).

Thanks to my son, Jamaal, for your patience, understanding, and love.

Thanks and appreciation to my mother and late father; my grandmother, Becky Scott; and my friends Dr. Wanda Fonte, Ph.D., and Harry Gillis, who sent their blessings from heaven.

Thanks to Candace Sandy for sharing her opportunities, time, ideas, and creativity. Finally, to Brother Roy Thomas, Randy Fong, Jean Stapleton, David Wells, Clem Richardson, Eva and Rasul Chew, Wayne and Georgia Williams, Mira Thomas, Dr. Marshall Hennington, Ph.D., Connie Aitcheson, George and Alicia Jordan, Marlene Bell, Wilber Farmer Jr., Yvette Rodriguez, Carlos Lozano, Joe Demma, Rich Galant, Lonnie Isabel, Les Payne, Walter Middlebrook, Ernie Sotomayor, Bob Keane, Dawn Kelly, Gillian Johns, Eva Duzant, Coretta Taylor, Mike Doyle, Terry Prettymah, Mark Toor, Sandy Banks, Jackie Jones, Lenora Pack, Al Stark, Dorothy Guadagno, Andrew Wills, Anthony Marro, Charlotte Hall, Beverly and Calvin Lawrence, Don Forst, James O'Neal, and the Legal Outreach students, thank you.

Foreword

WHEN **J**OEY **WAS ELEVEN** or twelve years old, he got a drum set. Right after that he got a turntable. He later earned the name of DJ Run. He was the fastest deejay I had ever seen. He was so fast that he could literally cut the air. Little did we know that Joseph "Run" Simmons would become one of the pioneering voices in the music and culture that came to be known as hip-hop.

To the millions of fans who are familiar with Run-D.M.C., you will not be disappointed. This spiritual memoir will share personal insights into one of the world's greatest rap performers. To those who are not familiar with Run, this book is also a must. It will allow you to get acquainted with a spiritual and socially conscious artist who has something important to share with you about living a more spiritually fulfilled life.

When he was about twelve, Joey got his opportunity to work as the disco son of Kurtis Blow as DJ Run. He came from a whole different aesthetic than any of the commercial rappers like The Sugar Hill Gang or the others out back then.

Joey as a kid always had a disdain for people who went the most obvious way. The reason that he, D.M.C., and Jam Master Jay dressed the way they did was because they wanted to make a statement about the community. They believed that the route they were following was really the guts of rap itself. It was not about being successful or about any commercial gains. It was about the new phrase, "keeping it real." That real attitude is what has given Run-D.M.C. the integrity to last for more than twenty years.

The first record that Joey participated in was *Christmas Rapping* by Kurtis Blow. He wrote the entire second half of the record and didn't get any credit. *"I am DJ Run on the microphone / a place called krypton was my home . . ."* Those were his lines. He never sued Kurtis, but that was his contribution.

If you listen to the first half of Kurtis Blow's *Christmas Rapping*, it was written as a very pop, commercial song. The second half, *"Throw your hands in the air,"* and that whole rap about *". . . came to the earth on a meteor, now they got me rocking on the mike,"* is really the epitome of what took rap from a marginal to a mainstream culture. Different from rock and roll. Different from jazz. Different from the blues.

Instead of crossing over because it became more acceptable, it crossed over because it took its guts and spilled them on the table.

Joey didn't get on MTV because he had made rap commercial enough. He got on MTV because he had taken it the other way. He made it less commercial, and yet at the same time he made it more acceptable and more commercial. In other words, he did the opposite of what the critics would have expected and the producers would have wanted.

He had to fight the producers, the record company, and everybody to do what he did. That kind of pioneering and belief in himself is what I think has triggered the entire culture into mainstream. In that regard, he is the biggest pioneer in hip-hop.

But, away from the world of hip-hop he is just as special. He is Reverend Run. As a brother, I can say that he was the leader of our family because he has such strong spiritual ties. He's got a direct line to God, while most of us aspire to talk to Him. Reverend Run can just call Him up with one ring. Whenever there is a time of hardship in the family we all look to Reverend Run for spiritual guidance. When my mother passed, although I am older, Reverend Run just took over everything, and he became the big brother. For every spiritual matter in the family he becomes the big brother.

Lots of time, I have to look out for him when it comes to worldly things like business and money. But in the real things that matter in life, he has got a total handle on them—kids, family—and a clear perspective on doing what is right. He remains rooted in family, friends, and spiritual beliefs. Those are the things that make him a leader.

In this book, Joey shares with you his journey to rap superstardom, the highs and lows along the way, and his philosophies and true appreciation of life. He shares advice that will help you get through difficult situations. He offers motivational quotes and action plans that will serve as inspirations to you or anyone who is searching for a better life.

If this book has any kind of relevance, or gives any kind of insight to the way that he handles his day-to-day operations—not his business or how smart he is as a hustler—but how great he is as a human being, then it should inspire everybody to greater heights.

Joseph "Run" Simmons's *It's Like That* is an inspirational and moving message from a giant in the hip-hop industry that will educate, motivate, and inspire you to move to the next level. Imagine having a dad that is a reverend and a rapper. Joey has got it all covered.

—**Russell Simmons,**
  founder of Def Jam records and CEO
  of the Phat Farm clothing line

IT'S LIKE THAT

INTRODUCTION

IT'S LIKE THIS. Imagine you're walking down the street and everything is going great in your life: You have a nice car, a big house, a beautiful wife and kids. You have money and fame. People are saying you're great. You are believing and loving every minute of it.

That was my life: Run, the rap superstar. I am a living example that dreams do come true, even for a kid from Hollis, Queens, who wanted to entertain people.

Then boom. Imagine that for no reason you start bugging and doing silly things that don't make sense. You slip, blame everyone but yourself.

Then you wake up years later and realize you've lost almost everything: your family, your money, your fame. The things being said now are not so nice. That was my life: my dreams turned into a nightmare.

This book is my story, how I went from being at the top of the hip-hop business, the best at the rap game, to rock bottom.

The king of rap, played by himself, my vision and blessings taken away.

I was able to stage a comeback by walking a different way and changing my life's flow by challenging my addictions and adjusting my attitude and actions, by being down with the king.

The purpose of this book is to help show you how to change your life's flow and reach the full potential that is in store for you. Here, I will share with you my thirteen rules on how to stage a comeback from hard times and restore your vision and vitality. Oftentimes I have learned it is not just about being successful but also about living with your successes, which sometimes can be just as hard as living with your failures.

Run's House Rules will teach you to regain your self-confidence and self-respect and the spiritual energy it takes to make you whole again. You will also receive tips on how and what it takes to reinvent yourself and rise to the top of your game.

I will show you that you don't have to be a victim or loser, no matter what your circumstances. There is a spiritual victory to be had in changing your life's flow and putting yesterday's failures behind you.

By sharing my personal failures and spiritual victories I hope I can motivate and challenge you to fulfill your own spiritual destiny not just in the world of hip-hop but in all areas of your life.

I hope it serves as a road map on how to get up and get going by taking a chance on yourself, taking charge of your life's direction, and accepting the challenge to take a spiritual walk this way.

1

WALK THIS WAY

. . . So I took a big chance at the high school dance with a lady who was ready to play / It wasn't me who was foolin' because she knew what she was doing when she told me how to walk this way / Talk this way . . . / walk this way / Talk this way. Walk this way . . .

—Run-D.M.C. with Steven Tyler and
Joe Perry of Aerosmith,
"Walk This Way" (*Raising Hell*, 1986)

YEAH, I was the king of rap; there was none higher. And I had all the trappings that came with the throne: drugs and alcohol, women and money. All fueled by my insatiable thirst for mo' sex, drugs, and cash.

Addicted.

And I couldn't stop getting high on the lifestyle and power that come with being at the top of the rap game.

I'd check into a five-star hotel near the Los Angeles airport; the rooms were $750 per night, the best money could buy. There would be five, ten, sometimes even twenty women trying to get on the floor or hangin' around the lobby trying to meet, greet, and get a glimpse of Run, not just the rap star but the king of rap.

And, I must admit, I loved it. I basked in the attention, knowing that this was crazy. The groupies waiting in Chicago, Atlanta, Detroit, Dallas, and New York seduced me into thinking it would never end. Name a city, and the ladies were there waiting; limos lined up to ride; thick, $5,000 gold ropes to represent; and my uniform: Adidas, a sweat suit, and a black hat.

Thousands of fans turned out to help Run-D.M.C. rock the house each night.

And why not? Our sound was fresh, innovative. People had never heard anything like it. Compared to our beats—blazing guitar riffs teamed with the skillful vocals of me, Run; D.M.C. (Darryl Mc-Daniels); and Jam Master Jay (Jason Mizell)—all the others were just sucka MCs. We were the best showmen in the business. Sitting at the top of the rap game.

And, because of our exciting style, we ruled the record charts, the first rap group to sell millions of records. And we were just kids.

Crazy. Mad crazy.

And at eighteen I had the loot to prove it.

But God has a way of getting your attention. Almost overnight, mad confusion set in and things began to change. I began to slip. Our new record didn't meet the high expectations. The film we produced with our own money bombed. And although the new record still sold more than a million copies, I felt like a failure because it didn't do as well as the previous one.

With my head all messed up from smoking too much weed and all the pressure that comes with being the king of rap, my live perform-ances began to slip. I was being pushed to do shows at less than 100 percent. I needed a break, but kings don't take breaks; they rap on.

I couldn't find Run, and the fans seemed to stop coming. Although the arenas were nearly filled, the fans seemed to know something was not right in Run's house.

I neglected myself, the people around me.

I had lost almost everything.

My throne was being snatched away like a thick gold chain by a subway thief. I knew I had to do something, but what? It was like chasing after your gold chain: You knew that no matter how fast you ran after the culprit, you were never getting your rope back. So why bother?

There was no way out. I was trapped.

I couldn't find Run.

Intoxicated by the illusion of power I had created, for the first time in my life I felt as if I were failing.

I had lost my vision and my reason to live.

Lifeless.

I found my self-confidence to get through the day increased with each joint I smoked. The more I smoked, the more I found Run. So I smoked all the time.

I bought new cars, Rolex watches—anything flashy to make me feel and look like the king of rap. The problem was I didn't have the money or energy anymore to fuel the lifestyle. I did anything to avoid facing the pain inside.

But when your world is all about consumption, you're only going to consume yourself in the end.

Nearly broke, all screwed up, my vision blocked, I didn't have the strength to make it through another day. Being depressed was the lowest point of my life. Maybe I was suffering from a nervous breakdown, but there was something going on when I was on tour.

During this period, I can't say I was a willing participant in Run's world, but thankfully, although I didn't know it at the time, God was always with me.

Out of nowhere Bishop E. Bernard Jordan and Zoe Ministries appeared. I know it sounds crazy—and it was crazy—but there God was knocking at my door offering to bring me in from the cold.

I didn't listen at first. I couldn't see. My vision was blocked. I enjoyed the money, the cars, the ladies, and the fame too much. I was the king of rap.

In the end all those things weren't enough to fuel my soul. It was only after hitting rock bottom that I was forced to change.

I found Run, but he was not the same Run. He had been born again, spiritually empowered as the Reverend Run.

The spiritual transformation started in 1986 while I was out raising hell.

RUN'S HOUSE RULE

No. 1

You Get What You Put Out

You can't stay hot forever. What goes up will come down. No matter how big you get in the game, you will eventually come back down to earth. But remember, when the excitement and celebrity eventually fade, you were a class act before it all began. Change is a natural state of being. It will happen, so be prepared. Stay humble and remember when things settle down to earth it's only part of life's natural process of regenerating itself. Like a flower blooming, something new has to grow. And remember, you reap what you sow. You get what you put out.

It's Like This . . .

- Never forget: What goes up must come down. Stay humble.
- Be prepared for change. It will come.
- Life will kick you in the butt if you are not living right.
- It's part of life's natural flow when things settle down.

THE WORD: "Make a joyful noise unto the Lord, all ye lands. Serve the Lord with gladness: come before his presence with singing. Know ye that the Lord he is God: it is he that hath made us and not we ourselves: we are His people, and the sheep of His pasture."

—PSALMS 100:1–5

REVEREND RUN: "Almost overnight, mad confusion set in and things began to change. . . . I bought new cars, Rolex watches—anything flashy to make me feel and look like the king of rap. The problem was I didn't have the money to fuel the lifestyle. I did anything to avoid facing the pain inside. But when your world is all about consumption, you're only going to consume yourself in the end."

2

I beg your pardon? This is Run's muther—in' Garden!
—Run-D.M.C.
(sold-out Madison Square Garden concert, 1986)

IT WAS THE SUMMER OF 1986. Run-D.M.C. was headlining a thirty-city tour. Los Angeles, Chicago, Atlanta, Saint Louis, and New York City—and Madison Square Garden—were just some of the stops on our tour.

Several months before, we had released the *Raising Hell* album. And we were hot. It was Run-D.M.C.'s third album, but it was the sound that introduced the world to hip-hop.

We made a lot of noise coming out with *Sucker MC's* in 1983. And we had combined rock and rap music with *Rock Box* in 1984. But our fans knew us for our signature song and first big hit: "It's Like That."

That was until we dropped *Raising Hell*. Then things got crazy.

"Peter Piper," "You Be Illin'," "My Adidas," and one of the first major crossover rock-rap songs (and a video), "Walk This Way," with Aerosmith, hit the radio.

Overnight, we blew up. We were all over the place—the covers of magazines, MTV videos—wearing our trademark sneakers and black hats.

We were headlining the bill, above L. L. Cool J, Whodini, and the Beastie Boys—the hottest acts of the day—selling out night after night.

The three of us—me, Jam Master Jay, and D.M.C.—rocked every stage we hit.

Onstage, I was Run, the raunchy, dynamic, microphone-throwing Michael Jordan of hip-hop.

Offstage, I was respected and out of control, smoking weed and loving the ladies. It seemed like in each city there was more weed to smoke and more women available. And not just for me but for anyone associated with the tour.

It seemed the longer we stayed on tour, the more money we made, the more I grabbed at stuff that was not good for me. I was creating problems for myself. The lifestyle didn't fit my inner voice or morals, but I was handling my business, rocking the house each night. So what if I was high most of the time?

Nobody said anything. Why should they? We were selling millions of records; it was a culture where it was acceptable, almost expected, that you would have the ladies, smoke joints, drink. It was part of the tour.

When you are paid thousands—sometimes seventy-five thousand to one hundred thousand dollars a night—to perform it's hard to deal with your personal demons. It's hard to convince yourself something is bothering you. That something is draining you of your entertaining self.

When the tour pulled into New York, I was all for raising hell.

I remember pulling onto Seventh Avenue and looking out of the limo and seeing young kids, a lot of thirteen-, fourteen-, and fifteen-year-olds, in lines wrapped around the Garden.

We drove up to the back door, and I went into the Garden walking past the security people, and they were a little bit in awe. They were treating me like I was really big. I was feeling it.

A twenty-year-old, on my way to being prosperous and rich.

I was in a daze, because I was huge in there. But I was also really comfortable, because I had played there before the Fresh Festival and all. I was starting to feel like a veteran.

This is Run's house! I thought.

I went backstage. I had my own dressing room.

I was excited, a veteran. I went out and peeked at the crowd. They couldn't see me, but I saw all those kids in the house.

Run-D.M.C. had this routine where I would come out and say, "This is Run's muther—in' house."

But this night was different. Special.

Before going onstage, DJ Hurricane said, "Why don't you say, 'I beg your pardon; this is Run's muther—in' Garden!' "

"Tonight," I said, "I walked in here and they wouldn't let me in the back door."

The crowd, crammed into every square inch of Madison Square Garden, went quiet, listening to my every word, like I was E. F. Hutton.

I looked at security.

I looked at the door.

And the crowd was waiting.

And I said, "I beg your pardon? This is Run's muther—in' Garden."

The crowd went wild! I knew I was in control.

This was "Run's muther—in' house."

Me, D.M.C., and Jam Master Jay had this thing under control!

I prowled across the stage waving the mike. I was a maniac when I performed, out of control.

"Whose house is it?"

The crowd was in a frenzy. "Run's house!"

We played a couple of songs, I don't remember which ones, and the place was rocking. The energy was crazy.

I remember looking out over the audience, feeling like I was on top of the world. I could see people everywhere, all shades, rocking to the power of Run-D.M.C.

I saw myself controlling the microphone. I was the king of rap, and it was like me and the crowd were one. The kids were feelin' me. At the spur of the moment—things were at an all-time high—I had everyone in the whole Garden lift their sneakers in the air.

The spotlight was racing across the crowd, and twenty thousand pairs of Adidas were raised.

Everybody was goin' crazy!

I looked backstage, and there was this executive from Adidas standing there smiling. He knew about the song, had listened to the song, but this was the first time he was feelin' it.

"*My Adidas! My Adidas standing on 2-5 Street. Funky fresh and cold on my feet . . .*"

A sea of three-striped sneakers slowly waving back and forth like white leather clouds was raising a new roof at the Garden.

That summer night, it was Run's house. The lights came on, and I walked off the stage.

"Run! Run! Run!" The crowd was still wanting more of our music.

Backstage, the Adidas representative came up to me to say that Run-D.M.C. would get its own line of clothing if he had anything to say in the matter.

My own Adidas sneaker? The fans' reaction at the concert? I was in a haze.

Incredible. Months later Run-D.M.C. signed an endorsement deal with Adidas for something like $2 million.

But backstage that night, I was just humble. Dee and Jay were feelin' it, too.

It's like we were just doing our thing and the people accepted us for it. We knew we were big, but we also knew we were humbled, because we had worked hard, performed for free at parks and small clubs around the country, and slept in the backseat of our road manager— and now-legendary rap producer—Larry Smith's Caddy to get to shows.

That night, we blew the joint up. Raising hell in Run's house along with the Beastie Boys, Whodini, and L. L. Cool J.

We were given our respect, and everybody was happy.

I think about it often now, that night. I remember it like it was yesterday.

I got into the limousine by myself on the way home, knowing I might soon have my own line of clothing. I was twenty years old.

Crazy.

I was living a crazy fantasy.

On the way home to Hollis, Queens, I told the driver I was getting my own signature sneaker. I told him about the concert and the lines of kids wrapped around the building to see us perform. I told him the story about "My Adidas" raising the roof at the Garden.

I told him about my dreams coming true.

We got to my house and I tipped him $100. I was on top and I knew it. The king of rap, I could afford it.

I woke up the next morning and as my father opened the newspaper—I don't remember which one—I saw myself, Run, standing out front in a picture. It said: "Beat Box: Run-D.M.C. delivers an action-packed performance at the Garden," or something like that.

I looked at myself.

"Hit it, Run. Hit it, Run."

I am back onstage in command. At the time, Doug E. Fresh was the beat-box MC. The beat box was a side thing for me. But there I was onstage just hittin' it off Jam Master Jay's beat.

I had all areas covered. It was not like I was limited. I felt my rap skills. I didn't rhyme. I didn't say a word, just hit the beat box, in the photograph.

I was thinking I was the all-around guy. The flyest rapper. I was rhyming, hitting the beat box; everybody loved Run.

Black jeans, white Adidas with black stripes, black sweatshirt, and a $5,000 gold rope that Jay bought me.

I was the character Run. The epitome of cool.

There was nobody larger. *Sucker MC's call me sire.*

It was crazy. And I was watching it happen.

It must be the grace of God; I was thinking I was back onstage. But actually during the concert I thought everything but that. I knew God helped me.

I thought I had done something good at that point. I had worked for years to gain the MC skills, starting out at twelve; then I was known as the Son of Kurtis Blow.

But I wasn't thinking about God like I do now; I just thought because I had tried to be a good person, rapping was the blessing. Now, years later, I know you see God when you see people who are doing their thing.

That night I was doing my thing. There was none higher.

A maniac in control onstage. Whatever I told the kids they did. "Wave your hands. Take off your sneakers." They did it. What a very powerful thing, I think back now: Adidas sneakers were giving birth to a new era in music, rap, hip-hop. Three guys from Hollis, Queens. The epitome of cool: black hats, no laces in our shoes. Fans screaming, "Run!" at the top of their lungs. Kids wearing Run-D.M.C. T-shirts, sweatshirts, and hats just like ours.

When we started out and I told people we would someday have a hit album and sell out the Garden, they called me crazy.

"There's no way a rap show will ever be able to fill the Garden."

Naysayers.

But there I was, proving them all wrong, kids screaming for my best friends, Dee and Jay, the character Run the rap superstar. It couldn't be us, but it was. This was real.

We were happy. Just thoughtful, young kids.

But the Run-D.M.C. phenomenon was selling out arenas from coast to coast, performing at Live Aid and Madison Square Garden.

We were on the cover of *Rolling Stone* and *Spin* magazines and the first rappers on MTV.

Us, the crew from Hollis. From 197th Street. From 205th Street.

It was crazy.

No end in sight.

It was like that.

RUN'S HOUSE RULE

No. 2

Dreams Come True

One of the most powerful things you can do is have faith in yourself. Dreams are real and can happen, but it all starts with believing in yourself.

When I was growing up I had this dream of becoming somebody famous. I didn't know what I would do, but I continued to dream and work hard. Then I got into rapping and my whole life changed.

People would say negative things, but I just kept believing in myself. It didn't happen overnight, but it did happen.

It's Like This . . .

- Your mind creates your world and only you can change your mind.
- Any thing you can imagine or dream up you have the abilities to accomplish.
- God is talking to you about your life's mission. Are you listening?
- There's no way that you can bring about change in your life unless you can imagine and truly see yourself as you want to be.
- Once you get control of yourself, things and people around you will fall into place.

THE WORD: "And he that sent me is with me: the Father has not left me alone, for I do always those things that please him."—JOHN 8:29

REVEREND RUN: "But I wasn't thinking about God like I do now; I just thought because I had tried to be a good person, rapping was the blessing. Now, years later, I know you see God when you see people who are doing their thing. . . . When I started out and I told people we would someday have a hit album and sell out the Garden, they called me crazy."

3

THE SON OF KURTIS BLOW

Unemployment at a record high / People coming, people going, people born to die / Don't ask me because I don't know why / But it's like that and that's the way it is.
—"It's Like That" (Run-D.M.C., 1984)

THE WHOLE RUN-D.M.C. PHENOMENON had happened almost by accident. Believe me, I never could have guessed that I would end up a rap star when I was growing up because there was no such thing back then. Hip-hop was something that happened on the playgrounds, in parks, and at parties. There was no big money. There were no movie deals, record contracts, or endorsements. There was nothing but guys on street corners and in alleys beating on trash cans or whatever they could find.

For me, it started around 1975 while I was growing up in the Hollis, a neighborhood in Queens, New York. Every day my friends and I would get high on weed. We'd do the beat boxes, and we'd just begin to rhyme. Most of the time we would be in the alley getting high, rapping and rhyming and banging on something to get the beat. That was our music.

Back then it was me, D.M.C., Butter Love, Runny Ray, and Terrible T. We called ourselves the Hollis Crew.

All day long, every day, when we were permitted, we would just be rhyming and making beats in Dee's basement. Two old beat-up turntables—one was his mother's and one was his. We used his mother's stereo system and bought a Gemini mixer.

We didn't have a lot of records and mixing and the technology wasn't like it is now, but we had some beats. There was this album out then called *Super Sperm* that we would use to mix "I Can't Stop," "Disco Nights," "Super Disco," "Breaks," "Blow Your Head," anything that sounded good. Back then the most important rule of rapping was to use whatever was available.

The first place I learned to scratch was in Dee's basement. The first studio for the music of Run-D.M.C. was in Dee's basement. The basement was important because it was the only place where a turntable and mixer were available. This wasn't just about making music but about hanging out with my buddies.

And that was me growing up. Nothing flashy. I was just an average kid trying to have fun. My routine was simple: go to school, come home, shoot basketball, and go hang out with the crew to get high and rhyme.

The key to the Hollis Crew was doing something: playing basketball, smoking a bag of weed, or rhyming. It was like, "Do you have some money?" Get a dollar and we could go get a bag of weed. Our first mission was to get high. Yeah, we still had all the other responsibilities like homework and household chores, but once they were done, we would get some money to buy a bag of weed and either shoot some hoops or rhyme in the alley.

I think it was more than just us getting high. The fellows in the Hollis Crew were real people I could relate to.

Butter Love was the comedian. Man, he could clown and make you laugh. And he simply had the best jump shot on Hollis Avenue. Period.

Runny Ray was just a good friend. Special. He is still down with Run-D.M.C. today. He is well protected, well taken care of. I have bought him lots of cars. He is a nice guy. Part of the family.

Terrible T lived up the block from Dee, and I went to his house a lot while we were waiting for Dee to get home from school. Terrible T was always cool. I mean he was always neat. If we were smoking a joint, he didn't want the ashes to touch him. He would take forever to smoke a joint. I remember one time he took a long time to roll this perfect joint. We were all thinking, *The joint looks good, but you used up half the bag of weed.* But T was always neat. He'd have on a stocking cap because he had to have waves, and the girls loved him. If he was smoking a joint, he didn't want his eyes red. Imagine that: He wanted to get high, but he didn't want red eyes. He would put in drops.

It was while hanging out with the other members of the Hollis Crew that my self-esteem and confidence began to grow. It wasn't like I didn't have any confidence, but everyone needs a platform to display or develop his talents. I liked hanging around with the crew because they accepted me. I had friends on my block, but it was always like they didn't appreciate what I was about. Maybe in their eyes I was played out or something, but every time I would hang on my block it was like my friends there were always putting me down. If I was playing basketball, it wasn't like, "Nice shot." There was always something negative.

When I was hanging out with Dee and the crew, we would laugh and have fun. It didn't take long for me to start ignoring the people on my block and hanging with the people who appreciated me for the right reasons. I didn't have to pretend, just be myself. The neighborhood, the basketball courts, and the alley became my stages, my live theater, while I was growing up, where I found my first audiences.

Back then I had a reputation, like Butter Love, for going around making everybody laugh wherever I went. I was a good rapper, and I was funny. Even to this day, when I am not trying to be funny people will laugh. Sometimes when I am talking to my wife, Justine, I have to tell her, "I am not trying to be funny right now," and then speak. When I was cracking jokes in school and rapping all the time, I never dreamed that I was creating a career for myself. But I got to the point where I was getting better and better and started doing little performances here and there.

Back then, like our performances, our rhymes were basic. Everything was about a sucker MC or who was the best rapper. There was this basic rap format, where an MC would improvise and rhyme about his personal greatness over a beat track. It was like "Roxanne, Roxanne" and "Rapper's Delight." The music was there and some basic scratching.

Our sound was based on combining rhyme with music and the energy of the crowd. Our rhymes had style, precision, and energy. I would start the rap, and Dee would finish it. And then we would switch or say separate parts of the rhyme, creating def vocals. And there was Jay, the ultimate jam master, just pumping the beat and doing his thing.

For us, as our music grew it just wasn't enough to have a dope rhyme. We also had to have the drums, heavy rock guitar, or even an organ matching what we were rapping. It was all a sound, and as it is today, we got from the energy of the people. I think if you go to one of our concerts now and watch the fans, you will see that with our energy we give a good show.

One of the most popular rappers of the day, Kurtis Blow, was good friends with my brother Russell. This was when Russell, who is seven years older than I am, was just starting Rush Productions and putting it on the map. He would book rappers, and Kurtis was a superstar back then. "The Breaks" was a smash hit. Since Russell and Kurtis were tight, Kurtis came over a lot. Sometimes he would sleep at my house. They had met in college, where Kurtis Blow was starting to build a name for himself like Russell.

When Kurtis came around the house I would come out and rap. I had a little bit of skill at the time, and Kurtis was always down with giving me pointers and stuff.

I knew I wanted to be down with Kurtis, so I started DJing and scratching. A lot of what I did was patterned after Kurtis because he came to the house and we were cool. He kind of took me under his wing, and from there I just evolved into being Kurtis Blow's DJ. I started performing under the name the Son of Kurtis Blow.

Kurtis would get on the mike and do his thing, and eventually I would also get some time on the mike. You have to understand when rap first started the MC would talk to introduce the song or to get the crowd pumped while the music was going. So you would get: "Throw your hands in the air and wave them like you just don't care." But with Kurtis Blow there was always extra excitement. He was smooth. He not only had the beats, but he also had the lyrical skills to rap over an entire record, skills that allowed him to carry a crowd for an entire night. It wasn't hard for me to get up there and rap, even with my limited skills, after watching him and practicing.

I would play Dee some of the stuff I did with Kurtis, and then we would do some of our own stuff.

Russell had another friend named Rudy Sply. And he was around the house talking one day, and I was running my mouth. I was about twelve years old. This was maybe the spring of 1979. We were in the backyard cooking or something, but Rudy was in the kitchen talking with Russell and then I just heard it.

"DJ Run!"

It was the most special thing I had ever heard.

It was the coolest thing I had ever heard.

It was the craziest thing I had heard in my life, and I couldn't believe it had come out of his mouth.

It was because I was always running my mouth. One of Run-D.M.C.'s most popular songs is "You Talk Too Much."

"Twenty-five hours, / eight days a week, / thirteen months out a year is when you speak. . . . / You talk too much. / Homeboy, you never shut up."

Rudy and I were cool. I was this kid talking too much and having fun with Rudy talking trash. But now I had a new identity. I was DJ Run, sorta like Superman or Spawn, the new superhero, only nobody knew it yet.

DJ Run!

I saw Rudy in the city a while back, and he wasn't doing too well. I gave him some money, and we talked for a while. I told him he was very appreciated.

My brother Russell was by this time a promoter throwing parties everywhere in New York. I was the guy who put the fliers up in Queens. There were shows all over New York City and other places.

Back then, you have to remember, rap music was a lot simpler. The money wasn't there. The music wasn't in stores like it is now. Most of the time you could buy a homemade tape for a couple of dollars on the street. We would be drinking Old English and smoking weed. It wasn't just a Harlem thing or a Queens thing. It was just whether somebody had a tape and some weed. We didn't care; we were just having fun hanging out and banging out our music.

Russell's homeboy Spudy said to my brother, "Man, Russell, you better get with these kids, your brother and Easy Dee [as D.M.C. was known then]—they're off the hook. These kids are amazing!"

By the time Dee and I had graduated middle school we had become best friends. In high school Dee was going to Rice in Manhattan, and I was going to Andrew Jackson in Queens. Dee was into drawing and stuff, and Jay and I were into basketball, although Dee and I didn't hook up with Jay until after high school. I knew Jay from playing basketball.

So Dee and I were developing a close bond—almost like we were brothers. It was crazy. He'd say one word and I'd say another. We were becoming like one mind. When you see two people like the Las Vegas–based magicians Penn and Teller or two guys singing together in a doo-wop group, that's just how tight Dee and I became and remain to this day. Dee is someone I shared my dream of becoming a rap superstar with, and he appreciated me. Our special bond was one of the foundations of our rap style and music.

Russell started feeling me as an MC, but there was something he didn't like about Dee. I think Russell didn't like Dee's delivery or his look. I told my brother that Dee was a great writer. But Russell didn't believe in Dee being down with me.

I finally said to Russell, "You know what? If I can't be down with Dee, I really don't want to make records."

I twisted Russell's arm and he finally agreed to put Dee down so we could rap together. We officially became a group. We still weren't called Run-D.M.C., but we were a group. We would perform for Russell in the living room while trying to get our style down.

As we got better, we moved from the house to free shows. The whole first year of the group's existence, our career was a series of freebies. We absolutely loved what we were doing—and have never stopped loving it. Back in the day, we would be fighting over the mike in the parks with everybody out there. We had an energy that said, "Let's do this!" With time we learned to pass the mike back and forth and created our own style of rhyming that no one had ever heard before, with me starting a rhyme and Dee finishing it.

That unique style became our trademark. We loved what we did, and I think that was the key. It wasn't work. It was hard, but it wasn't work. We were just doing what we loved . . . and then things started to happen on a different scale. We already were successful and prosperous because we were just being ourselves. But then we were blessed with a different level of success and prosperity. We got a record deal. We started performing shows in places like Wisconsin and other parts of the country where people had never even heard of rap music.

I can't really remember where our first paying gig was because we performed so many shows for free. But I can tell you when the people started feeling us and we knew we had something special. We were in North Carolina, at some sort of promotion for a radio station.

Jay used to walk around with this boom box. So we were walking to the dressing room and Jay was playing this little beat he had put together, and some of the people in the crowd heard it.

Everybody started screaming and going wild. It was dark out, and maybe several thousand people were starting to go wild.

We were maybe eighteen at the time. It was winter and "Sucker MC's" was hitting hard.

We arrived and Jay walked in bumping to his beat on his boom box. We were thinking we were sneaking in, and the people heard the beat and they completely lost their minds.

You know the three of us were wondering what was going on. This was cool and we were thinking we were about to tear the place up. We couldn't believe that the crowd was going crazy.

On our *King of Rock* album, we did "Jam-Master Jammin'," and the rap goes: *"Couldn't wait to see Jam-Master Jammin', couldn't wait to see the master jam. / His name is Jam Master, / call him Jay, / the crowd goes wild when he starts to play. / Everything is correct and A-OK. / Jam-Master is on the move but his sounds will stay."*

Well, it was crazy for Jay, because we hadn't even started rapping and the crowd couldn't wait to hear his beats and our rhymes.

We got to New York, and we were performing at the club Danceteria, or something like that. The crowd was almost all white, and the sound was new to everybody. The patrons heard our beats, and the crowd lost it again.

I mean crowds had lost it in North Carolina and again in New York, and we were rapping for different crowds and people just lost it.

How we dressed was just as innovative as our sound. Run-D.M.C. pioneered a whole new way of dressing. We would have on sweat suits and black hats and unlaced Adidas. It was funny how we got that look. Jay was responsible for our dress code.

It was around 1984 and we were making money, and Jay bought whatever he wanted. One day Jay wore this incredible outfit. He was walking down Jamaica Avenue, the main shopping drag in Queens, and he had on all this expensive stuff: leather pants and a leather jacket, Adidas, a big gold rope, a black hat, and some Gazelle glasses. Everybody was checking him out, because he had on everything that everybody else wanted. (Jay could afford everything because we were making about fifteen hundred to two thousand dollars each for every performance. And we were working hard for the money. We could do two shows in Brooklyn and two shows in Queens and Yonkers all in the same night if we started around 7:00 P.M. and things were scheduled right.)

You might see somebody with a rope or some Adidas or some Gazelles but not every one of them on at the same time. Jay was walking down Jamaica Avenue and it was like everybody wanted to snatch something from him because he had it going on. I mean nobody had everything: the glasses, the leather, the shoes, and the gold rope.

So we were doing well and Jay just was helping to create a nationwide trend and didn't know it.

Russell later refined the look by matching everything up so the appearance was cool but neat. But it was Jay who first influenced our look.

When the albums blew up, so did our look. Almost every young person in America tried to emulate us in some way. It was unbelievable. I don't think Adidas has sold as many shoes since 1986, when the song came out.

But my childhood was more than just us rapping. I think what made all of the success easy for me was the love I received from my brothers, Russell and Daniel Jr., and my crew.

My parents were very good to me, too. My father, Daniel Simmons, was always my role model. He worked for the New York City Board of Education as a college professor. He was the reason I first started writing poetry around age eleven. He was my early inspiration. And he always supported what I was about on some level. We always had a relationship where we could talk. Same with Russell, Daniel Jr., and later the crew.

Growing up in Hollis was special. Nice homes, manicured yards, and everything. But it wasn't like we were sheltered from the world. There were some places where we could still see the drug dealers on the corner.

My father, my brothers, and the Hollis Crew made it OK to be Joey. It was like before there was the Son of Kurtis Blow, DJ Run, Run, or the Reverend Run I was just Joey Simmons from Hollis. And well, that was cool, too.

Things were good and we knew it. The worst thing was when we couldn't rhyme or play basketball, but most of the time we were able to do our thing.

Even today, I love making a good rhyme and keeping things simple. It just feels right to scratch and come up with something.

In 1983, our first single, "It's Like That/Sucker MC's," which Russell produced, became a hit. Success flowed like water: television interviews, magazine covers, packed arenas from coast to coast. All the people who said we'd never make it were eating their words.

Everything came in a whirlwind: Fame. Money. Drugs. Sex. Women.

I didn't know it at the time, but in Run's house it was the calm before the storm.

RUN'S HOUSE RULE

No. 3

Keep It Simple

Some of the best things in life are very plain: playing basketball or cards or taking a walk with your family. Take time to enjoy a quiet Sunday afternoon or the lyrics to a new rap. In this fast-paced world, things can get complicated at times. But remember, the best things in life are free and easy.

It's Like This . . .

- The best things in life are always simple. Enjoy them.
- Get excited about living. The world is such a beautiful place.
- Once you get control of yourself, things and people around you will fall into place.

THE WORD: "Take therefore no thought for the morrow: for the morrow shall take thought for the things of itself. . . ."

—MATTHEW 6:34

REVEREND RUN: "But my childhood was more than just us rapping. I think what made all of the success easy for me was the love I received from my brothers, Russell and Daniel Jr., and my crew."

4

RAISING HELL . . .

*Kings from Queens from Queens comes Kings / We're rais-
ing hell like a class when the lunch bell rings.*
—"Raising Hell" (*Raising Hell,* 1986)

WE WERE MAKING hip-hop history with our third album, *Raising
Hell,* and I was feeling confident and strong, like I owned the world. I
was truly the king of rap, setting trends, winning honors, and selling
millions of albums.

When I performed I was the illest of all time, Run. He was raunchy
and fun, the great entertainer. The problem was when Run came offstage, Joey Simmons the man was buggin'.

But still I was happy, enjoying the spotlight, lovin' everything. My
life was great. But the signs of trouble were on the horizon. I was doing
my thing. I was probably doing stupid things, but at the time I didn't
know it. Just as quickly as I had shot up the charts, I was feeling much
love: from my family, my fans, the band. I was feeling like I was a winner. Big Run from around the way, nobody cooler, you definitely
wanted to be me. I was young, raising hell, and selling millions of
records. I was also planting the seeds of destruction.

Women everywhere. There was this dude on the road who dressed
up just like his brother. All he had to do was put on the hat and girls

would flip. He probably was getting more girls than his brother. On any given night you could walk into the hallway of the hotel and there would be topless girls running from room to room. Getting girls was no problem for Run; I was the king. And I knew it. I now know that wasn't the way to go. But back then I was a kid at Toys " Я " Us and there were enough skateboards to go around.

One big part of Run-D.M.C.'s success was our catchy rhymes that made you think or sometimes laugh. No violence or harsh language, just thinking, laughing, and having fun.

I like to laugh and I like to make people laugh. There is a song we called "You Be Illin' " about the strange stuff people do in normal situations. Part of the song talks about a guy who goes into KFC and orders small fries and a Big Mac, instead of chicken; in another part of the song a guy goes to a basketball game to watch Dr. J score and screams, "Touchdown!" Just illin'.

Like the song, I was illin'. Only it wasn't funny.

As I told you before, we were headlining with L. L. Cool J, Whodini, and The Beastie Boys.

Run, prowling the stage, throwing the microphone, was rocking the house and taking care of business.

At the hotel, Joey Simmons was raising hell.

I didn't know it at the time, but God was trying to talk to me. The partying and performing night after night kept me too busy to listen, though. I was having what I thought was fun. But the lifestyle was taking its toll.

Right after the *Raising Hell* tour ended, things began to change.

I was still smoking my weed. I couldn't stop smoking weed. It almost became like a god to me. One day I came into the city to see Jay and his man Randy, and when I got to the city Randy said, "You got some weed?" and I said no and he said, "How the hell did you get to the city?"

They knew I had to smoke a joint. They knew I couldn't get from

Queens to the city without smoking a joint. It was like grass was my fuel, the weed I needed. That's when I knew I had a problem.

While I was trying to kick weed we began to record *Tougher Than Leather*. And we were talking about making *Tougher Than Leather*, the movie.

Me and Dee made a vow not to get high, but we both fell off.

Then it happened. Something grabbed me. It changed my outlook on everything. Even to this day I can't explain it, but it was some kind of deep depression that took over my life. And for some reason I stopped being a happy person, enjoying life, and began feeling like the weight of the world was on my shoulders. But I was the king of rap, so my depression didn't make any sense.

It seemed like there was no way out of my depressed state. I absolutely didn't care about anything. It was just so deep that I was suicidal for no reason. Nothing mattered. *"Get me out of this spell I'm under—this mind-altering spell*, was all I could think. I felt like I was trapped in a horror movie like *The Exorcist*.

It's painful for me to think about it, even today, but I wasn't the only victim. Like me, everybody falls on hard emotional times. Imagine you're going down the block, you're happy because something good has happened in your life—a baby, a new job—everything is going great, and in an instant your whole world comes crashing down.

Boom. It hit me. The bottom fell out, and before I knew it I was stuck in a deep depression.

Illin'.

I was going crazy. I was a normal human being, doing well—a successful young man. I felt like somebody had put a year's worth of voodoo on me!

I wasn't caring about anything. I couldn't keep functioning like that, so I began subconsciously yelling for help. Like most people, I wanted the pain to end quickly.

The success of our biggest album at the time, *Raising Hell*, was over, and here we were Run-D.M.C. on the verge of dropping a terrible album and movie at the same time.

After the megasuccess of *Raising Hell*, which was certified four times platinum with several top-ten singles, our next two albums were considered flops and we were getting dissed by everybody (even though our albums sold in the millions).

During the 1988 *Tougher Than Leather* tour things ground to a halt. We didn't sell out the 20,000-seat arenas; only 12,000 people came out. That meant that we didn't surpass the 4 million that *Raising Hell* sold. Kids didn't love the *Tougher Than Leather* album or movie. It was unrealistic for me or anybody else to expect the album sales to continue at the rate of *Raising Hell*, but my thought process was all screwed up.

Tougher Than Leather wasn't selling, the movie was a flop, and, worse, I was being pushed onto the road to tour. Run, the personality, was still in demand.

Something inside me was saying, *You don't want to succeed.* Some crazy stuff. I stopped eating. I stopped calling my family.

With my fame slipping, I became more and more anxious. I wanted to stay home. My imagination and my visualization powers were not there. Run may have been Superman, but Joey Simmons was barely hanging on.

Couldn't anybody see it? Everything was going to hell and I was locked in my hotel room, tripping for no reason.

I was on tour with Public Enemy and Jazzy Jeff and the Fresh Prince (Will Smith), and instead of enjoying the ride, I was locked in my room. The Fresh Prince was happy. Public Enemy was happy to be there.

But the great Run was out of energy.

I slipped.

I'd say things like, "I really don't want to drink a glass of water. What for? Why do I want to sustain life when I really want to die?" That's how messed up I was.

Like I'm thirsty—but why drink when I'm trying to commit suicide? I asked myself, *What the hell are you trying to live for? Why do you want to live and drink this water when you really want to die?*

I had no—absolutely *no*—thoughts of going forward with life.

I was not Run. I wasn't even smoking weed then. Smoking weed—for what? I was suicidal! It was crazy.

My inner conversation—my zest for life and greatness—had stopped.

Whether it was from energy that other people were giving me or from what, I didn't know. But all of a sudden I was out of it. And it lasted for a long time.

Dee and Jay knew it. "Look at Joey," they said. I was not happy-go-lucky and making jokes like I usually was.

Two weeks before the tour I told Russell that I didn't want to go out. He sent me out anyway. My behavior didn't make sense, and there was money to be made. We were still the biggest rap group on the planet. And I was still the king of rap. There had been deals made and there were commitments to live up to, so Russell almost had no choice but to put me on the road.

The whole tour I did not perform up to par. I was just out there. Everything was normal as far as everybody else went.

People said, "Get up and fight, Run," but I didn't want to get up and fight. I was hurt. I wanted to lie down and die! I was being pushed to go on tour because it was always make an album, go on tour, make an album, go on tour. I couldn't get off the treadmill if I wanted to.

One evening when I stepped off the tour bus with Dee and Jay in Houston, I came to the conclusion that my whole spirit had been ripped away from me.

But I did not have the will to just say, "Forget all this! I'm going home!"

My depression was fueled in part by the decision to make the movie with the same title as the *Tougher Than Leather* album. We messed up big-time when we decided to make the movie using our *own* money. I found out the hard way that nobody makes a movie using their own money.

When the movie and album failed, our reign as kings began to end. After years of ruling supreme, it seemed that everything we touched was no longer turning to gold. We no longer were the men of the moment, no longer poster b-boys for the American Dream.

Money became an issue.

Things got worse.

To top it all off, in 1991 I found myself in an Ohio courtroom battling charges of rape that were totally ridiculous and untrue. At the trial I learned a woman had sat in the front row of our Cleveland concert, enjoying the show. After the show, women were all over the hallways at the hotel, our usual scene. The woman from the front row showed up at the hotel with a group of her friends. While her friends hung out at the hotel, the woman left, called the cops, and said she had been raped by me.

Like we did after every show, if we didn't have to perform the next day we went home. So, back in New York, I was at dinner when Big Dee, my manager, called me on my cell phone and said, "Yo, some girl in Cleveland said you raped her." Suddenly I was no longer hungry.

I was in shock.

Meanwhile, cops searched the hotel room and found condoms, marijuana, wrapping paper, and other stuff. It just didn't look good. The next thing you know, I was indicted.

Later the truth came out and I was cleared.

All of this, of course, cost me hundreds of thousands of dollars in legal fees to clear my name. I didn't even know who she was, but I still had to spend the last of my real money on the case, which was thrown out of court.

I came home happy, but my wife was upset.

Despite the evidence showing I was innocent, my wife thought that I had been unfaithful.

Back at home, the tour was over and I was trying to live a normal life again. I tried to get past my depression and start over. But I couldn't pick up the pieces and put them back together.

My wife took our kids and left. It wasn't just the stress of the trial. Our relationship had been strained for a long time.

So, with my marriage over, I was looking to steer my life in a new direction.

While all this was going on, the new album, appropriately titled *Back from Hell,* was in the stores.

It flopped. Panic began to set in.

My heart wasn't in it. I was just plain tired.

Something had stolen my light, and I couldn't seem to get it back. It was then that I started realizing that maybe I had been grabbing for the wrong things in life.

The fame, money, and women weren't ending my depression or getting me closer to being Joey again. Or the real DJ Run.

I got down on my knees and prayed, but nothing happened.

My ego was in overdrive. I was in denial. I continued to chase material things. I wanted more, the best out of life. Why, I don't know, but I figured I was number one and nobody was better than me.

I prayed some more, but neither God nor anyone else seemed to be listening. I couldn't even understand myself, so why should anybody else?

It was not my intention to ignore God, but I had given up my spiritual power to worldly things and not to God. I had not been thankful for my success. My overinflated ego had led me to believe I was the man—better than everybody else.

When you start believing the hype, God has ways of bringing you down to earth. I learned the hard way.

I was spiritually bankrupt.

Emotionally spent.

For the first time in my life hard times set in.

My musical and financial successes were no longer enough. I realized there was more to life than material gain. I needed something more.

I needed for the pain to stop. Life is not easy when you're all alone and faced with the dark realities of your existence.

I was afraid of the dark. And sometimes fear makes you do things you wouldn't otherwise do.

It made me turn to God.

Now I was ready to listen, ready to learn.

The lessons began.

RUN'S HOUSE RULE

No. 4

You Will Make Mistakes!

Sometimes they will cost you nothing, and other times they may cost you everything. But you can survive them. Accomplishing anything requires trial and error. So don't worry about making a mistake. Focus on accomplishing your goals. Visualize and dream. You will make mistakes, but you can survive them if you stick to it. And remember tomorrow is a new day filled with new opportunities.

It's Like This . . .
- If you are trying to accomplish something, you will make mistakes. It comes with the territory. If you don't want to make mistakes, don't do anything.
- Don't expect something for nothing. Be willing to show God that you really want a better life by working harder when problems arise.
- Don't let a temporary setback force you to quit. Success is just around the corner.
- God will test you to make sure you really want what you say you want. Some of the results are called mistakes.
- Don't allow the frustration and pain caused by a mistake to force you to give up just when your blessing is about to arrive.

THE WORD: "All we like sheep have gone astray; we have turned everyone to his own way; and the LORD hath laid on him the iniquity of us all."

—ISAIAH 53:6

REVEREND RUN: "I didn't know it at the time, but God was trying to talk to me. The partying and performing night after night kept me too busy to listen, though. I was having what I thought was fun. But the lifestyle was taking its toll."

5

SPIRITUAL HARD TIMES . . .

Hard times spreading just like the flu / Watch out, home-boy, don't let it catch you / P-P-Prices go up, don't let your pocket go down / When you got short money you're stuck on the ground / Turn around, get ready, keep your eye on the prize and be on point for the future shock / Hard Times.
—"Hard Times" (*Run-D.M.C.*, 1984)

■ **TOOK MY OWN LIGHT.** I took my own light by not living up to par.

No one could come and take my light, because I was so big I could only do myself in. Run-D.M.C. always had our place, and we always kept our street credibility. Even to this day I only care about what the kids on the street are saying. Only after the street gives me its stamp of approval do I care what everybody else has to say. And we basically created the whole game. But no matter who you are, after greatness comes the day of doom. You've got to pay the piper. A few years before, we had found the perfect way to combine hard-core b-boy attitude with a rock-and-roll feel. Our style made us seem more real than the rest, quite unlike the groups that came before us. The other groups went onstage looking like the Village People, wearing wack costumes with feathers and frills. We laughed at them, with our hard-core style. But now we were no longer the flavor of the month. The bottom line was that Run-D.M.C. just wasn't that hot anymore.

And, sitting in the dark, I was now ready to listen to the teacher teach. One of my first lessons came in the form of another rapper.

As always, L. L. Cool J and lots of other rappers were trying to take over our spot. But L. L. Cool J was a different challenger from the rest.

L. L. Cool J was always one step behind us. His whole career was like one year we'd love him, the next year we'd hate him. L. L. was always giving us a strong run for our money. When we were on the *Raising Hell* tour, he was on it with us. There was always a rivalry between us and L. L. It wasn't like he was stealing our spotlight, because he was going through his own thing—ups and downs with the rap game. But L. L. was always there, lurking nearby and not in the shadows.

We were always having a battle with L. L. At the top of our career, during "Walk This Way," L. L. made "I Need Love," and that went to the top of the charts. He was always like Hercules fighting three guys—Run-D.M.C.

I say L. L. is like Hercules because there was really nobody else who could come close to fighting us. L. L. is a strong guy, and I think about this almost every day. Not L. L., but being of strong mind. L. L. had gone through so much, with seeing people getting shot in his house and things with his father. L. L. wasn't even from Hollis, but he would claim Hollis just the same. In my mind it was always me, Dee, and Jay against this one guy—L. L. And he would really fight hard. I would say, "How can anyone withstand this power of Run-D.M.C. and all of Hollis?" L. L. was loved; however, he never had that total street love like Run-D.M.C. But he didn't let that stop him. He would come so strong that he'd be right there in my face and people would be loving him.

We were so powerful when compared to L. L. because we had everybody from Hollis on our side. I wouldn't get chased around the neighborhood and stuff. But to L. L. he was always an underdog—and that was what was always so great about him. Even to this day, anybody who ever messed with L. L. in one way or another got into a whole lot of trouble spiritually. Even Canibus, a rapper who just came out a year or so ago. Canibus was the new flavor and was supposed to be beating L. L. But L. L. didn't even have to beat Canibus on the mike; he just put out a wack album and *beat himself.*

Kool Moe Dee was supposed to be battling L. L. at one point and just got knocked down, too. There's something about L. L. He just knocks things out of the way. I don't know how, but the bottom line is Canibus was new and now he has no career. Neither does Kool Moe Dee (in case you didn't know).

L. L. was just always there standing tall. All you can do is respect that. He came up two years after me. We did "Sucker MC's," and he did "I Need a Beat." He was on Russell's label, Def Jam. And L. L. was a smart guy. He studied Run-D.M.C. and, with his own style, grew into a monster. He'd sit in a room, lock the door, and just study me. Like the master MC that he is, he was trying to figure out the source of my power, my light, so that he could take his game to the next level. At one point, he even thought my power and appeal was in my *sideburns!* Seriously.

I guess the best way to describe him is as a boxer—just a really hard-battling guy. There's no beating L. L. because he'll just still be there throwing his blows.

So there Run-D.M.C. was destroying challengers, including L. L., but suddenly I didn't care about being the so-called king.

I was able to watch things being off-balance, but I still didn't care. I was out of touch with family members whom I used to confide in, including my father. Childhood friends who weren't connected to the music business had been replaced by a stream of publicists, radio programmers, promotion men, managers, other musicians, and fans. Lots of fans. They all wanted a piece of me. There was no time for recreation—much less *introspection*—and I was falling apart, little by little. I was overbooked and overcommitted to everyone except me. I was no longer doing the things that had kept me focused and fulfilled all those years growing up—routine rituals like playing basketball with my friends, sitting down having a real meal with my family, and going to church on Sunday. I was empty inside and searching for some true substance. I can truly say this didn't happen to me because I was in the entertainment industry. It happened to me because I let it happen. Just like it could happen to anyone: a police officer, a physician, a CEO of a major corporation, or a housewife. We can all get off-track, and while it may be to different degrees, the result is still the same—spiritual burnout. Call it what you want to, it's all the same.

And when nothing is working, sometimes the best thing that can happen is having that magic carpet snatched out from under you, falling on your face, suddenly going from walking in peace and tranquillity to the eye of the storm.

Sometimes it takes time for mistakes to surface. But the seeds of stupidity that I had sown had finally taken root and grown up to be a big, dumb, foolish weed. And just as it took time to take root, it would take time and effort to chop it down. The more you've sown and watered your seed and let this weed grow, the harder it will be to pull up the root. The weeds of unhealthy relationships, habits, and beliefs are hard to prune. But unless you do, you can't plant new seeds for success. It is a law of nature. Once again, you have to pay the piper.

When you're off-base, you really don't believe you are going to get in trouble for the way you are living. There's no reason to change in your mind. You feel like you deserve everything. I mean you can feel empty and not admit it to yourself. That's where you get stuck. It's called *denial*. But in the back of your mind there's a little voice—no matter how dim or weak—telling you to prune the weeds that you tend to ignore. Some call it intuition. Others call it conscience. But I call it

God. A little voice that grows into a roar over time telling you not to prune but to remove the weed.

It was time for change in my life, but I just didn't know what direction to move in. I was in a cycle of lustful living fueled by money and ignorance—too weak to remove the weeds, but smart enough to know something had to be done. And when you are in that position, you are normally surrounded by people, drain people who are pouring buckets of water on the weeds trying to continue to feed off the fruits of your labor. Listen, as far as lustful living goes, there will always be drain people around trying to suck you dry. Because they are so motivated by their worldly desires, they won't even realize when you move on or know they're empty. But one day you'll come to a place where the music stops, the bankroll ends, the party is over, and the lights come on. Things are no longer what they were. That's your opportunity to start looking for the blessing, because then your vision is no longer blocked by the trappings of the world. It's hard to look back while a lot of things are happening, because you're so distracted. For me, my distraction was being a so-called star, but it could have been anything. Succeeding in life no longer concerned me. I was so crazy and depressed that nothing mattered.

No other creatures on earth but humans get off-track like that. I mean a tiny mustard seed knows its potential and path from day one. It doesn't hold onto doubts or anxieties as it develops and grows. It knows what it is. It stays on point, steady, consistently stretching upward in an ever-changing world that is sometimes harsh and hostile.

When I was rapping, every time I got onstage it wasn't until the moment I opened my mouth that I was able to rid myself of the fear that dominated every moment of my life at that point. So I always felt like I had to "perform." Even in my everyday life I was putting on an act to hide my fear. I was confident in my abilities as a performer, where I was in control, but in my day-to-day life I was falling apart. I had to make a change.

You might feel like you're buried in the dirt right now. Do you ever feel the way I felt—like you're on a perpetual treadmill, running harder and harder and getting nowhere fast? You know where you want to be in life, but it's just not happening the way it's supposed to. Or you're trying to figure out which way to go, but each turn seems to lead to a dead end. Do people say you're "successful" while you are still feeling empty on the inside? Remember, that's the way I felt at the height of my success. When I was on tour, I was being pushed to do shows where I couldn't even be 30 percent, much less 100 percent.

You know what I'm talking about if you are in a relationship, but you still feel alone. Or if you are working overtime every chance you get and still barely scraping by from paycheck to paycheck. Or if when things are going great for you, you count the days waiting for everything to fall apart.

A lot of times we complain about how life isn't going the way we want it to but feel like there's nothing we can really do about it. *It's just the way things are,* we say to ourselves. *Grin and bear it. There's nothing you can do about it.* Right? Wrong! Whoever you are and wherever you are in life, regardless of what anybody tells you, it's never too late to reinvent yourself. It's always in your power to do so.

Reinventing yourself means realizing that at your core is a valuable treasure. Years of dirt may be heaped on top of that treasure, so you may have never seen it. Or you may have discovered it a long time ago only to have forgotten it was there. But it's there. It's the gift from God that we all have within us whether we know it—or remember it—or not. I think of it as a diamond.

I didn't know it at the time, but the depression had started my journey to uncovering that diamond, or my natural spiritual power. It would give me the strength to pull up my weeds and claim my legacy of self-empowerment and spiritual enlightenment that comes from being down with the king. It led to me being a born-again Christian. It also led to me being a minister. But more important, it led to me understanding my spirituality and developing a closer relationship with God. I learned to work with a good and pure heart to uncover the treasures I have to give to the world.

There was a time in my life when you couldn't have told me that I wasn't perfect. The world was mine, or so I thought. I thought I was *all that*. But the problem was I was actually still in training. I had some grit, rock, and substance, but I was not a diamond yet. I couldn't see my own flaws and imperfections, no matter how big they became. And, like most people, I didn't like to face the facts. We've all done something that we're ashamed of, and I was ashamed of a lot of things that went against my upbringing, which contributed to my low self-esteem. And with the low self-esteem you are afraid to claim what's yours out of fear of embarrassment or failure. Part of my becoming a minister was to embrace who I was becoming. To do that I had to truly examine my worth. I needed to find out if I was a real natural resource, a precious mineral, a diamond, or just another fake on the horizon.

Have you ever seen those late-night infomercials for diamels and cubic zirconiums? They're supposed to look just like diamonds, but they only cost $29.99—and you get a free bracelet if you call before midnight! But what's the difference? To the untrained eye they look just like the real thing. Although I was the real deal, my lifestyle had taken away my spiritual strength, and I was the cheap imitation of something valuable. At first glance I was a beautiful shining gem, but up close at the time I was cubic zirconium, a tiny splinter of glass that is left when something breaks. My spirit was broken.

When you enjoy life and you do things in moderation, then you're more appreciative of life. If you are speeding, then you miss a lot and crash and burn. But if you drive at a reasonable speed, not only do you increase your chances of getting to where you want to be safe and sound, but you'll be able to smell the flowers as well.

I was a superstar caught up with living an illusion that was causing me to miss out on the greater things in life. And everybody can get trapped in this, whether a superstar or not. You can miss talking to your mother and father like I did; you can miss having a relationship with your children. You can miss the true blessings of life. And you can get to the place where you can't really enjoy what you do have.

If it gets bad enough, pretty soon you don't even respect yourself. You can end up building your own little world. That's what I did. In your make-believe world, you're the most important person. You can get caught up in seeing the same faces every day and start thinking that your world is everything. This can happen to anybody. In your own world, you give yourself an inflated sense of self-importance. As soon as you start thinking, *It's all about me*, you're in trouble. You never leave your bubble, and all the people you see every day treat you like the emperor who has no clothes. Everybody knows you're screwed up, but nobody will tell you. Nobody will help you because they either are just as messed up or don't want to stop the gravy train. Everybody knows you're walking around naked and making a fool out of yourself, but they just go ahead and let you. I was surrounded by thousands of people, but I was all alone at the same time, if you know what I mean.

Still, I kept hearing that voice inside telling me that I had something more to give. That I was special, a unique treasure waiting to be found. A beautiful diamond waiting to be displayed. You heard it before, but there is a valuable treasure inside you when you stop chasing after illusions. When you start keeping it real. It can only happen when you quiet your mind for a minute and when you begin to listen to God, because He is always speaking to you.

God had whispered and then started yelling at me to listen. But the higher up you go, the further down you have to fall. It doesn't matter who you are; the universal laws of nature dictate that when something takes you very high and drops you, you fall with the same amount of force it took for you to rise.

Realizing this will help you heal things that you didn't even know needed healing. It will make you unafraid to confront the demons that you'd been avoiding for so long. When we came into this world, we didn't know fear. Fear is something that we *learned* through years of reinforcement inflicted on us by others. People with good intentions are often too busy fighting their own personal battles. They didn't want to see us hurt. They tried to protect us, but in the process they loaded us down with generations of burdens. Those burdens are what keeps the diamond buried inside us.

Once fear enters your mind-set, it attacks your heart, mind, body, and soul. It takes over and keeps you from growing spiritually. That's why it's hard for a lot of people to believe there is a great treasure inside them. To find and uncover the valuable treasure, you first have to believe in your heart that it's there waiting for you to claim. You might not know how to look for it or call it forward at the moment, but you know it's there, a blind faith and belief system that tells you your diamond is there waiting to be uncovered.

Uncovering that diamond is the reinventing-yourself process. You first have to be able to see the new you in your mind's eye. A lot of times we complain that we don't have what we want, but we don't even know how what we *say* we want is supposed to look. People say they want to be successful, but they don't even know in their minds what success looks like. There's no way that you can bring about change in your life unless you can imagine and truly see yourself as you want to be.

That is where prayer comes in. Prayer is imagination. If you don't know what your blessing looks like, it could smack you in the face and you wouldn't even know it. Prayer is imagination; imagination is prayer. I totally believe that in my heart. God is inside you. God is not somebody sitting there making decisions in the heavens saying, "Now I am going to give it to this person and not to that person." Prayer helps to shape your mind and aid you in visualizing what it is that you should be doing to uncover that diamond. What image do you have of yourself? What image do you put before your subconscious mind? Stop trying to impress other people and impress yourself. The first person you need to impress is yourself, because when you impress yourself other people will be impressed, too.

People see you as you see yourself. If you come in looking all meek and scared, people see you like that. However, if you look at yourself as powerful, that is how people are looking at you, too. The bottom line is: what you see is what you get. The key to reinventing yourself is seeing things in a new light, seeing yourself being successful.

As a result of seeing the new you, "problems" or obstacles in your life become opportunities for self-improvement. Instead of being negative circumstances, they become transitional steps toward your goals. The hard times with no money or places to go become opportunities to stay at home and meditate on things you need.

Everyone should reinvent themselves. You have a mission in life — whether you know it or not—that's your buried treasure. You must always remember that obstacles don't hold you back; *you* hold you back! I might never have seen what I truly was if I hadn't reached the depths of despair that I reached. I might never have known God if I hadn't lived the life that I've lived.

When you realize that God has been and always is talking to you, you'll appreciate the Bible verse: "All things work together for good for them that love the Lord and are called by his purpose." You'll realize that even the worst things that have ever happened to you were really all for your own good and that you can make it through. You won't even appreciate what is on the other side—and you won't value it— unless you go through a serious process of committing yourself to bettering yourself. Understand that you can't go wrong, because God is in your corner. The proof is the fact that He has brought you to this book.

Do you ever wonder why people are so fascinated with the idea of buried treasures? I think it's because it's so amazing to us that something so valuable could come from something so common and messy—so unwanted by anybody—as dirt. But it's a kind of hope that we all try to hold onto. Not long ago I was at the point where I literally felt like my life was dirt and mud, unclean, and the furthest thing you can imagine from being a treasure. You know what I mean if you've ever felt like everything in your life was an absolute mess.

There's no way around it—digging up a buried treasure is *dirty* business. It's not like going to the jewelry store in the mall and picking out a pretty diamond in a glass case. No, diamonds are buried inside massive amounts of dirt and coal. The work takes place miles under the surface of the earth. The more off-base you are, the more work it will be, like finding a needle in a haystack. You've got to persevere and be patient even when the whole thing seems pointless. Sometimes it's hard to keep going because you're so caught up in instant gratification. You want everything and you want it all right now. If you want to uncover the diamond that's within you, then you also can't be afraid to get dirty dealing with all the things in your life that you've been trying to avoid. And you can't be afraid to go underground for a while. I completely dropped off the face of the earth for a year when I was getting my life together. During that time almost nobody was able to find me. It's easier to just stay "clean" and never deal with the dirt, but then you never really get anywhere. And remember, even if you were able to go to a jewelry store, you still would have to have earned the price of a diamond.

I was once watching a program about Silicon Valley and its entrepreneurs. Several of the people being interviewed said there are two kinds of people who say they want to be millionaires, those who want to spend a million dollars and those who want to make a million dollars. At one point I was, like most people, definitely in that "spend" category. I just wanted to be rich. I'd be perfectly happy if I could just hit the lottery and get rich that way. I didn't care how I got rich. Like the millionaires in the program, we need to put one foot in front of the other and learn how to march toward what we want, learn how to set goals and plan our future.

You have to learn to enjoy the process that brings you our blessing instead of just wanting the end result and not caring about anything else. You have to enjoy digging for diamonds.

When you do find joy in bettering yourself, you will put yourself on the right track—you'll know where to dig, and you'll know the diamond is down there. And you won't give up when you get tired. You'll keep going because you know how much effort God put into creating your diamond in the first place. If He put so much into creating that diamond inside you, why aren't you willing to meet Him halfway by working hard to bring it out?

Most of us give up digging for our treasure when we are just a few inches away from it. We get tired of trying to pull those weeds. That's just the way life is. There's always a sense of questioning whether you're doing the right thing when your blessing is just around the corner. This is God's way of testing you to see if you really want what you say you want. There's going to be a lot of coal and dirt to sift through. You're going to be looking for a tiny gem in the midst of tons of things that you don't want. But that treasure has the power to change your life. And you are the only one who can decide whether or not you really want it.

Creating a change in your life calls for making yourself God's partner in the process. A raw diamond is a gift from God, but the all-important job of cutting the stone is in your hands. A million-dollar diamond can lose value in an instant if it's cut incorrectly. God is the professional craftsman. But your eyes are the eyes of God. And your hands are His hands. We have to allow ourselves to be divinely guided by Him.

Just like anything else, the universe will only help you if you help yourself. God can lead you to water, but He can't make you drink. If you say you want to make a change in your life, God will have a way of testing you to see if you're really serious about what you say you want.

When you cut your diamond, you'll be shaping your talent and abilities and all that God has given you—making it work for you. Every time you look at another person with jealousy or envy at what you think he has you're off-base. We are all given gifts, not the same gifts but valuable gifts, each in its own way. Our mission is to figure out how to best utilize our gifts to better ourselves and everything around us. When you do what you're supposed to be doing, you don't have time to look at anybody else and be upset at what he has or what he's doing, because you're on-target with your own mission. Cutting your diamond is about honing your gifts. Whether it's being good with children, being a great artist, being a great comfort to sick people, or enjoying dancing—we all have gifts that we neglect. When we neglect the gifts that we are given, they are taken away from us because apparently we don't want them. They're just like muscles: if you don't use them, you lose them. But again, if you take one step toward what you want, it takes two steps toward you.

A lot of people have been running from their true purpose in life for a very long time. Maybe you are doing that because you're rebelling against what everyone always expected you to do. Maybe you've just been so caught up in surviving from day to day that you haven't even thought about it. But no matter what, make up your mind what you want, because, as a wise person once said, "whatever you really want, the whole world conspires to bring it to you."

I should also mention that the company you keep plays an important role in reinventing yourself. It's cool to go in your closet to meditate and pray, but if as soon as you come out you are surrounded by people who turn you off, then have you really found the diamond that is within you? When you realize the value of your relationships, you'll cherish those people around you because you'll realize that each of them is there to show you something about yourself.

When I came to God, I got so excited that I wanted the whole world to share the joy that had come to me. I wanted everybody to see my diamond. When you become excited about something, you can't keep it a secret. There's an old church song that goes: *"Couldn't keep it to myself,"* in reference to the joy that God brings into our lives. If you are truly on a collision course with disaster and death and sin, and God comes into your life and turns you around, you will be like me and others who have experienced God's goodness: You won't be able to keep it to yourself. Everything you do will be a testament to the new you. You will be so happy that joy will just come bubbling out of you without your even asking, like a beacon of light and hope.

No. 5

Reinvent Yourself

You have a mission in life whether you know it or not. Don't let obstacles hold you back; *you* hold you back! Problems are really opportunities for self-improvement. Learn from your mistakes, meditate, make changes, and move forward.

Remember, people see you as you see yourself. The key to reinventing yourself is seeing yourself in this new light, seeing yourself being successful.

It's Like This . . .

- It's never too late to reinvent yourself. And it's always in your power to do so.
- Prayer is imagination; imagination is prayer.
- You can only beat yourself. You can only take your *own* light.
- You have to know that there's a new you inside if you ever want to be able to find it.
- The rich take chances while the poor play it safe.
- It's not all about you . . . so stop thinking it is.

THE WORD: "For thou art my rock and my fortress; therefore for thy name's sake lead me, and guide me."—PSALMS 31:3

REVEREND RUN: "Reinventing yourself means realizing that at your core is a valuable treasure. Years of dirt may be heaped on top of that treasure, so you may have never seen it. . . . It's the gift from God that we all have within us whether we know it—or remember it—or not. I think of it as a diamond. . . . Uncovering that diamond is the reinventing-yourself process. You first have to be able to see the new you in your mind's eye."

6

WAKE UP

Wake Up. / Get Up. / When I woke up this morning and I got out of bed. / I had some really fresh thoughts going through my head / they were the thoughts that came from a wonderful dream, / it was, it was a vision of a world working as a team. / It was a dream.
—"Wake Up" (Run-D.M.C., 1984)

YOUR LIFE GOES IN PHASES. I was just a kid when Run-D.M.C. became successful. I started rapping when I was just twelve years old. I was very much into being number one. Learning how to handle fame and success can become a lifelong lesson if you let it. I didn't know that what goes up must come down. I didn't realize that I wouldn't always be on the top—that there has to be room for other people to come up and take over. I didn't realize that not being on top didn't make me a failure. In fact, it represented a time for growth.

Life goes in phases. I encountered fame at such an early age that it blocked my growth as a person. I didn't know what was normal, so I had trouble identifying life's natural course. When my first wife was finally getting ready to leave me, I was going through the same things that other couples might go through at age twenty-seven; the difference was I was in the public eye and everything was magnified. It affected the way my wife and I acted and communicated. And because

I was young and having so much come at me all at once, naturally there would be things I was not capable of handling. The problem was I just had too much on my plate, too much confusion going, to even give myself time to develop in the natural progression that it takes a boy to grow into a man. But it wasn't all my fault; there was just a lot of stuff going on.

For me, being number one had been everything. I was so demented. It didn't matter that I was failing or the 1988 album, *Tougher Than Leather*, wasn't selling. I knew it was a good album and we had done our best. "Run's House," "Mary, Mary," and "Papa Crazy," with a hard riff from the Temptations classic, were good songs with phat beats. And "Miss Elaine" was a fun song about a teacher making passes at a student. My attitude at the time was "get me out of this spell. Shake this depression and everything will be all right." When you're young, any little thing can set you off if you don't have patience with yourself. I had no patience, and I went down.

The album failed to meet my high standards and the expectations that everybody had for it. I thought I was the king of it all. Who was bigger? I thought I was da bomb. I thought Run could never make a mistake. At the time, God was trying to make me humble, but I was too caught up in being a "star" to even know it.

SPIRITUAL AMNESIA

Though I grew up in a religious home where we prayed daily and went to church every Sunday, after years of being on the road, consuming and looking outward for satisfaction, I developed what I like to call Spiritual Amnesia. Spiritual Amnesia is a state of mind that progressively takes over and clouds everything. I think it happens when a series of events overwhelms a person. Your behavior and actions change, and the amnesia sets in. You forget yourself.

I was ignoring my inner thoughts and not nurturing my spirit. And in doing so I was creating conflict within myself and with others. I was going against the values that had gotten me to where I was. I was going against nature. I'd been relying on outside things to guide me, instead of my own radar, my God-given abilities. I started out losing my self-respect, and it went further than that. It got to the point where I was near total destruction. *I had forgotten who Joey was and totally become Run.* I had no time for my wife or children. I had no time for my two brothers or friends. All I cared about back then was making money and being on top. I did whatever it took for me to hold onto where I was. I didn't want to go back. Now I know it doesn't make sense, but I didn't want to go back to being Joey.

From where I sat, I could've done just about anything. Instead, I chose to chase life's so-called finer things: gold watches, cars, women, and stuff. But I was neglecting the natural life force that sustains all humanity—my inner voice. God talking. You could say that's when the Spiritual Amnesia hit, and though I was at the highest point in my show-biz career, my soul was buried 100 miles deep in the earth. I was hit over the head with success, and I totally forgot who I was.

LOOK AT YOUR ROAD MAP

Out like a light, I began searching. Have you ever set something down in a house and couldn't find it? It might take a moment for you to remember where you left it or you might have to do some searching, but you do find it. Well, that's how I felt. I felt if I just kept looking, I would eventually find myself again. So I looked at the road map of my entire life: where I had been, where I was going, and why. Growing up, I was surrounded by love and had everything a child could want. When I was younger, my father transformed every day into Christmas in our house. I was the most spoiled kid in the world. I got whatever I wanted. In a strange way, I think that was a key part of my whole success in life—and also my failure—*I felt like I deserved everything.*

My father was a professor at Pace College, and he taught at night. There was a time when every single morning when I woke up and came downstairs I would see a brand-new toy sitting there for me. Every day I got something: bubbles, balloons that would make crazy noises when you let the air out. The gifts weren't expensive, but they were filled with love. I don't know exactly how long this lasted, but I clearly remember that every day I would run downstairs and get my toy before school. This feeling-entitled-to-everything mentality carried over into all aspects of my life.

My father used to tell me, "Joey, you never really had to pay," and now I think he might've been right. When I was younger I didn't understand what he meant. I thought he was joking. "Run-D.M.C. paid dues," is what I had always told people. We performed for free for years. We kicked down doors so that a new generation of rappers could get radio play and do shows in stadiums. We did shows in places people had never heard of. We performed shows where hardly anybody showed up. We stayed up all night perfecting our craft. We did whatever we had to do to get to earn our success. You couldn't tell us that we didn't pay our dues. But now that I'm older I understand exactly what my father meant. He meant that apart from Run-D.M.C., Joey the man hadn't had to sacrifice to have all the things that he received in life. I hadn't had to pay my spiritual dues, so to speak. My father wanted me to be confident, but unfortunately, I didn't learn to be humble in the process. He wanted me to have great expectations and to feel entitled to success, but you've got to stay grounded at the same time.

I was trapped in the materialism that I had grown up in. If something wasn't right, hey, buy something new. Every day is Christmas, right? Well . . . wrong! I was very depressed when I realized that I didn't understand the principles that really guided the world. I had no idea where to look for my diamond. Asleep at the wheel, out like a light, I was drifting in my Spiritual Amnesia, out of touch with the normal things a twenty-seven-year-old man should do.

Sometimes people tell me how they had such great childhoods and their parents gave them everything, so they don't understand why they have so many problems. I can relate to that. I had the most loving and nurturing environment, but I didn't get the values that my dad thought would just come naturally. It was too late when he realized that the love was the base, but the respect had to be earned. Of course I respected my family, but when you're put into different situations it's easy to lose sight of things that aren't totally ingrained in you.

My parents gave me everything. But there are some things in life you just have to earn yourself, universal principles that must be learned before you are allowed to graduate and move on to the next level in life. So the first place my road map led me to search was my beliefs or principles. The first thing I remembered was that if you want respect you have to give it. I had to respect the people in my life who deserved it.

Before you can respect others, you have to respect yourself. And that was the hard part. I had to find Joey. You have to be willing to go back as far as your childhood and look at the events in your life that helped shape who you are today. You may have had a terrific childhood filled with love and joy, or you may have a rocky beginning that you're trying to overcome. Whatever the case may be, your experiences shaped your personality, your character, and your whole life.

Before you can shake Spiritual Amnesia you must put your personal demons to rest. You will never be at peace or exist in harmony with the universe until the wars within are over. Those doubts, anxieties, and fears must be resolved. How do you do that? Well, the truth is nobody can tell you that. I can only share with you what worked for me and hope that it gives you a clue or a road map to get you started in the right direction. For me, I began to find religion.

WHERE'S GOD?

We are all molded in the image of God. We all have unlimited potential, meaning that's just the same way Jesus found strength in himself to go against the laws of the oppressive society he was living in and fight the power with what he believed. We all have what it takes to tackle the enemies in our own lives. We just have to go in and look for it, harness our inner power. This can only be done by telling ourselves the truth. God is not some painted image with long hair whose home is up in the clouds. God is real. He is inside me and you. He acts as our inner voice—a natural navigational system that guides us toward our true purpose. It is not about asking God what he can do for you. I learned it is looking deep inside to see what you can do for yourself. The key to me ending my depression and finding Joey again was inside me. I had the power, me, Joey, Run. It was up to me.

THE CHILD'S IMAGINATION

I knew I had been placed on this earth to do something special. We all have been placed here for a purpose. There is a reason for everyone's existence. We are born with a limitless potential to dream and the energy to turn those dreams into reality.

I remember when I was a kid I used to run around the house, arms outstretched, and imagine I was flying—defying gravity like a 747 or my favorite Saturday morning cartoon character. I created whole new alternative worlds complete with their own languages and customs.

Kids feel they're able to climb any mountain, cross any stream, go anywhere their hearts take them. Back then, no one could tell me there were any boundaries. The world was my playground. The pure innocence of magic, imagination, to play make-believe and express yourself in pure joy.

But now I had lost my joy. If you lose that innocence, your life changes. I had to reclaim my imagination, my childlike sense of adventure. I remembered the time when Dee and I were reading a children's book that had the line "dum didi dum didi didi dum dum." We loved that line, and that became the hook for "Here We Go," one of our most popular songs.

There I was trying to undo years of training and conditioning and starting to look for new ways to express the old me. The Joey way. People have always told me, "Don't do this," or, "You can't do that." Sometimes you end up choosing a path out of anger, fear, or some other emotion and it is not who you are. Search inside and find you.

Everybody—rappers, businesspeople, schoolteachers, sanitation workers, or whatever—is in search of peace. And it's a beautiful thing when we can wake up in the morning with that childlike eagerness about life—fully trusting that whatever happens, everything will be all right. Unfortunately, we're conditioned to believe that the quality of our lives has everything to do with outward things. So we buy that new flat-screen TV or the shiny off-road vehicle with the satellite navigation system or that regal condo in the tree-lined, trendy section of town and think it's going to make us happy. It's fine to have those things, but when we chase after material goods, trying to keep up with the Joneses, we usually think all those things are magic pills that are going to cure whatever is making us sick. But after the shopping sprees are over, we continue to feel overburdened and empty.

To fill the hole in the soul, some of us turn to alcohol and other drugs, but we continue to be unhappy because we crave conversation with our spirit. That's the thing that gives us our creativity, wisdom, and zest for life. A lot of people substitute addiction for real communication. What happens is everything gets twisted. We think we're having fun when we're really creating chaos. We swear we're being brilliant when we're really just running off at the mouth.

If you're not feeding your spirit, you will be left floating around aimlessly in a crazy ever-changing world. Until you realize that all the power to create the new kind of life you want exists within, your life's journey will seem more like walking down one dark alley after another, getting nowhere. The frustration will set in, then the depression.

Movies and television will bombard your senses with suggestions about how you should look, where you should shop, and what you should wear. But if you ignore your inner world, you give up the reins of your will. Little by little you'll get separated from your true purpose, until you become an empty shell of a person. Life will turn into a series of struggles between private thoughts and the public image you've created—the same way it did for me.

KNOW WHAT YOU'RE LOOKING FOR

If you don't know what you're looking for, one thing's for sure: you'll never find it! People get on their knees praying for God to help them, but they aren't really sure what they want God to help them with. When you know how you want your life to be, then you can make it happen. You'll stop begging and trying to coerce God by giving Him a wish list of things. Then you'll see God for what He really is—a universal spirit that helps you help yourself, the angel that sits on your shoulder whispering advice.

People think that praying is getting on your knees, maybe fasting, to convince God to move for you. Wrong. That's not what it's about. The line in the movie *Jerry Maguire* said it best: "Help me help you."

When Tom Cruise said that to Cuba Gooding Jr., I almost fell out of my seat, because I knew that God was basically saying that to all of us. That's what real prayer is all about: getting at peace with yourself so that you can allow God to move through you so your inner strength can be manifested.

It's definitely not about looking at what other people have and asking for that. That's the perfect way to get caught up. It's exactly how I got caught up in a life that I asked for. I wanted to be like all the other stars: going to premieres, riding around in fancy cars, having beautiful women on my arm and all the nicest things money could buy. That's what I asked for; I wanted to be a "star." And boy, did I get it!

You can't covet other people's things or lifestyles. You don't know what they're doing when they're not on camera. You can't see what goes on behind closed doors.

It's scary to me when kids say they want to be just like their favorite athlete or musician. When I talk to kids in schools I tell them to pick people they see every day to idolize and not someone they see on television, because they have no control over what part of someone's life they wish for. For example, you may say, "All I want to do is be like so-and-so," but you don't know what that person's life is about. If you say, "I want to be rich like so-and-so," at least you're picking a part of a person that you want to emulate. You might just say you want to be like a particular star and then end up being like him in arrogance, meanness, or something else that you didn't have in mind. You should pick the attributes or qualities of a person that you want to emulate, or else you may get the bad without any of the good.

A QUIET MIND

You have to go within yourself and say, "God's within me; let's go forth." You can't wait for God to make things happen. You have to take action, and when you do, your consciousness will change and you will be able to manifest miracles all day long. It's a process of solitude, and it's not as simple as it seems. Part of my problem was that I couldn't get things quiet.

Have you ever played the quiet game? The quiet game requires silence. You count to three, and then the person who stays silent for the longest period of time wins. It's fun with kids because they can't get past the second minute before they're wiggling and giggling and finally burst out laughing. That's all fun and games, but try it with yourself. The first time I tried just to sit in solitude and clear my mind of the rat race of my everyday life, *I* turned out to be the one who couldn't last for two minutes. I literally couldn't contain my thoughts. I thought about everything I did, had to do, or could do with the time I was spending sitting there being quiet. It wasn't an easy process to master, but I had to do it if I wanted to be able to have an honest conversation with myself! It is hard to break through the noise, but it can be done.

You will have to master this game, too. The simplicity of silence is the only way to find the hidden treasures within yourself. Try to sit with yourself every day for just five minutes. Silence. Clear your mind of all the things you have to do and all the things you want to do and just be still. You may not get up to five minutes the first time, but eventually you will. The less stimulation around you, the better. It's like being asleep but being awake at the same time. When you're asleep your body rids itself of all the impurities of the day. Your mind is in an unconscious state, but your body is working hard to rid itself of all the stress and waste of your day and heal. Now this is the time when you can sit with yourself and do this process for your mind. Without that inner peace for both mind and body there is chaos, and in a chaotic environment you can't be prepared for anything.

But everything takes preparation.

PREPARATION TAKES CHANCES

You must prepare yourself for what will most likely be a long haul. The Bible says the race is not given to the swift or to the strong but to the one who endures until the end. Your reward comes from enduring until the end. A lot of people put forth a good effort for a little while, but when the chips are down they give up. Exhausted, they say to themselves, "This is too much work." The bottom line is, if you want to dig for your treasure, you have to be willing to come up empty. There are no guarantees that you're going to always discover something new and wonderful about yourself. The difference between the rich and the poor is that the poor play it safe while the rich take chances. A "wealth mentality" understands that there are no guarantees in life. When you start trying to make a change in your life, you just put your best foot forward. If you're the kind of person who only wants the sure thing, then you'll never take a leap of faith in anything. You'll never do anything outside of what you're doing right now.

The key to what's not right about your life is not anything outside yourself. If you think about everything that you've experienced and that has ever happened to you, ask yourself what the one constant in all these things—good or bad—is. The answer is Y-O-U. You are the common denominator. When you realize that, you'll see that what you need to change is yourself and not anything around you. In fact, you'll go crazy trying to change other people and other things, because really you don't have any control over anyone or anything but yourself. Once you get control, things and people around you will fall into place and you won't have to worry about them anymore.

Have you ever seen people wandering around on the street looking lost and confused? That's what happens when you don't know that you have a treasure. You feel like things just happen, like you're not even in control of what goes on in your own life. You've become a *victim of circumstance*. Things come along and just seem to take over, and when it rains it pours. You don't even have to be an active participant to get mixed up in the wrong kind of lifestyle. Some people go unknowingly—just following the crowd to their own personal destruction. That's OK, because God still looks out for you. Until you get it, He's right there pushing you to get it. You may have to face the depths of despair before you figure out what's going on, but He's always with you. At my lowest, God was with me even then, but I didn't know it.

When you realize that the secret to everything that you want and need in your life is right inside you, that's when your treasure hunt begins. I had to learn that again.

X MARKS THE SPOT

Part of seeing your treasure is knowing you can achieve it, and part of achieving it is knowing that there's a different way. It will end up being easy to spot what needs changing in your life, like it was in mine, when you're truly ready. There may not be anything wrong in your mind about your life. But maybe you're too close to *see* what's wrong. Sometimes it takes those moments when everything hits the fan to make you finally get yourself in gear. Maybe you have to get outside yourself and see yourself as if you were another person. Ask yourself: Do you really feel like you're doing what you should be doing to be the person you need to be? Are you happy where you are in your life?

We defer our dreams with excuses and don't realize how it affects the lives of everyone around us. When you have an idea or there's something that you want to do, do you start making a mental list of all the reasons that it can't or won't work or isn't a good idea, or do you think of even *one* way that it can work?

When I started rapping, I knew it could work. But still I had to deal with the naysayers. You have to believe it can happen and create your own treasure road map to success. Map out the things you want to change in your life so you know what you're doing. I made the decision my depression was over. I just needed help in mapping out my course of action.

Have you deferred any of your dreams with excuses? Have you said to yourself, "I wish I could do that, but I don't have the time"? Write down all the things you want to do or have wanted to do. Look at each and every one of them and ask yourself what's stopping you, what's *really* stopping you. Part of your treasure is buried in the answers to those questions. Really examine your answers before you proceed. I thought what was stopping me from being number one was everyone around me. No one was working with me; they were just working against me. It took me a long time to realize that the only person working against me was me.

I had to really look at my health, my finances, and my relationships and every aspect of my life and get ready to make a change. Sometimes it seems easier to just let sleeping dogs lie. Sometimes it seems easier to just not deal with things if you don't absolutely have to. But unfortunately, that's not how you grow. It's like trying to sweep your house with a broom and no dustpan! All you end up doing is shuffling dirt from one spot to another—from the middle of the floor to under the rug—but you never really change anything.

Any way you cut it, digging means breaking new ground. It means being ready to sweat, be tired, and work underground in pitch-darkness sometimes. Obviously, it's easier to just stay relatively comfortable aboveground—to just put Band-Aids on what's wrong with your life instead of really trying to fix anything. Or to be a fake diamond, because how many people are really even going to know it's an imitation? But that's not why you dig for your diamond. You don't go after it for the world; you dig for it for yourself.

Digging will require the ultimate faith to know that the diamond you're looking for is there. What you are searching for is real, even if nobody else has seen it.

It's easy to have faith in earthly things. For example, every time you sit down in a chair, you have faith in the chair's stability and strength to support your weight. Unless the chair is visibly broken or unstable you don't even doubt that you'll be OK. Now you have to learn to have the same faith in God. God has the stability to always support your weight. Take the same type of faith that you put into things you see every day and put it in God. That was the key to ending my depression, knowing God was there. When I had faith that God was going to help me change my life, He did. Now I see God inside me. I don't look at God as a spirit sitting on top of a mountain up in heaven looking down at me. I look at God as being everywhere and in everything.

People see God when they let the diamonds that are inside them come out and shine. When people do their thing, they are showing their diamonds off to the world, showing off their version of God. Michael Jordan is "God" on the basketball court. Reginald Lewis was "God" in the boardroom. When I look at R. Kelly I see "God" in another form. When I look at "God" another way I see Wayne Gretzky. I see "God" through motivational speaker Anthony Robbins. Your faith has to be in the fact that there's something great inside you that is just itching to come out if you give it a chance.

The road that carried me to God wasn't always a smooth one. Who would've thought that I would be able to find God in the crazy world of hip-hop music? But that's just the way it happened for me. I was determined and I kept going and somehow I came through it all. I have been through hell, but today I'm back. I took control of my life, and once again I'm achieving. Only this time, it's a little different. I've learned some rules of life, and the secret to winning is putting everything in the right perspective. Basically, you can't allow external things to become more important than feeding your inner soul.

You don't necessarily have to be at the lowest point in your life to embark on the journey I endured. You just have to be open and willing to take the first step and to be guided by something other than your lusts and desires, a fundamental belief in something bigger than yourself: the principle to turn your life around.

Coming to God changed my way of looking at everything. I had been so wrapped up in getting and spending that I didn't know anything about giving. I always expected to get everything without giving much of myself—except maybe a performance. But then I only received material things, things that could always be taken away as quickly as they were given. But what I have now can never be taken away. With what I have now, material things can and do come, but my priority is faith.

You see, I'd always had faith in myself, my abilities, and my performance, but when I hit bottom I realized that faith in myself was not enough. It was a much larger faith that I needed to guide my life, and that faith was not something that could be seen. Back then I had faith in everything but God. But I hung in there and He brought me back from the brink. My faith helped me to find my hidden jewel and restore my life. If I can come back from hell, so can you.

You have to be true to yourself.

Live your dreams.

RUN'S HOUSE RULE

No. 6

You Are Always a Winner

I was out of control. Too much of everything. Caught up in the fast lane, I began my fall from grace. I had lost myself by doing silly things and not following the laws of nature. There are rules to the game of life. Pay attention and respect them and you have a chance to win. Ignore them and you will beat yourself.

It's Like This . . .

- In order to fix the outside, you must first fix the inside.
- God is an inner navigational system. When you listen, He guides you toward your true purpose in life.
- You have to know that there's a new you there if you ever want to be able to find it.
- Stop trying to twist God's arm to get Him to move for you. Ask not what God can do for you but what you can do to be the most God-like person you can be.
- Learn how to ask God for the right things.
- You see God when you see people who are doing their thing.

THE WORD: "Even so ye also outwardly appear righteous unto men, but within ye are full of hypocrisy and iniquity."—MATTHEW 23: 28

REVEREND RUN: "Though I grew up in a religious home, where we prayed daily and went to church every Sunday, after years of being on the road, consuming and looking outward for satisfaction, I developed what I like to call Spiritual Amnesia. Spiritual Amnesia is a state of mind that progressively takes over and clouds everything."

7

Down with the King

For the eyes of the Lord run to and fro throughout the whole earth, to shew himself strong in the behalf of them whose heart is perfect toward him.
—2 Chronicles 16:9

I WAS HIGH AS A KITE the first time I passed through the doors of a church called Zoe Ministries in New York City. The minister there, Bishop E. Bernard Jordan, who had never before laid eyes on me, put his hands on my shoulders and started telling me things I didn't even know about myself. He said, "I see success coming toward you in the air. I see prosperity. I see things turning around for you. You're in a season now of confusion. I see you searching, trying to find your way. You have not entered this place by mistake. The spirit of God has led you here, and I hear the spirit of the Lord saying to you that you shall rise up again. Things shall turn for you. You were on the right track once you walked through this door, young man."

He told me, "Get ready for a new life now!" It was at that moment that I realized what a terrible mess I had made of my life. Right there on the spot I broke down in tears. I was at the absolutely lowest point in my life. It was then that I knew God was listening and my life was headed for a change.

I believed I still had something left to give inside of me, that I was still a worthy person, but I couldn't lie: no matter what Bishop Jordan said early on, I had a hard time believing him. I couldn't find my light.

In order for me to survive, I had to do some soul-searching and find the real me, find out what really went wrong. Inside me I knew a good person was still alive. I was just struggling and fighting to get out.

I knew I wanted to live. I knew the real me was there; I was just having a hard time finding it.

My first move was to deal with my issues of denial. I wasn't being honest with myself and how I had been living. I knew what I knew, that smoking weed all the time wasn't really me.

Next, I had to learn how to separate the real Joseph from Run, or clean the dirt from the diamond. I had to let go of the old feelings and move forward. I had to let go of all the things that were not working for my benefit and restore some order back in my life. And, in doing so, I didn't know it at the time, but I was putting a divine force back into my life.

My change began late one night when I was watching television alone in my hotel while on tour. I came across a televangelist named Robert Tilton. Something just drew me to him, and I needed to hear what he was saying. He was up there, on the screen, talking about how when we forget God bad times come into our lives. I completely felt where he was coming from. At one point during the program, Tilton directed his congregation and the viewers at home to bow their heads, close their eyes, and pray. It was the first time I had looked inside myself in years. I looked around the big, empty, fancy suite, and all I could see was the television and the hallway light in the distance. The more I listened, the more I began to understand there was a divine force at work. I began to feel free, like the weight of the world was being lifted off of my shoulders.

I knew I needed spiritual healing and guidance. Sifting through the dirt for me meant learning to start appreciating what I had and, even harder, sharing what I had. Some nights I would go down to this one-dollar hamburger place near Chung King Studios New York, where we recorded, buy 200 hamburgers, and just give them away because I couldn't fill that void of emptiness inside.

After hearing Tilton, I knew I had found what I was looking for. Right then and there—on my knees in that dark hotel room—I made a promise to God that He would be a part of my life from that day on. Every journey begins with a single step, and once I humbled myself to something larger than me I was able to embrace change.

The Bible talks about separating the wheat from the tares, which are plants that look exactly like wheat when they first sprout. In order to determine which plants are the wheat, you have to let the plants grow to maturity.

Uncovering the truth of you underneath all the lies you've been told—and told yourself—can seem like an impossible task. And in truth, it's not easy. But like the tares and the wheat, if you give things time, you will be able to spot the right thing. All my soul-searching led me back to my roots. I had learned the lessons. It was time to wake up and stop blocking the blessings.

GOD IS INTO THE DETAILS

You can't be greedy. You can't be impatient. You can't just grab for the first thing you feel. There's no short-circuiting the process. You have to take the time to inventory what's happening in your life. I call it the process of making the "mess into a *message*."

It had taken a while for my mistakes to pile up and surface. It had taken a while for the seeds of destruction I had planted to take root. They were just small plants in the beginning. They didn't come up and try to choke me out for a long while. That's the way it always is. It seems like you can do whatever you want, and then almost overnight the bill is due. So from 1985 and 1986, when I was sailing on top of the world, the problems were visible but not considered major.

But by 1989 the problems had taken full bloom and I couldn't handle them. If I had taken care of them when the problems were small, maybe things would not have gotten so bad.

It is funny, because up to that point everything in life was so big for me that I didn't have time to learn anything about the truth of myself—or at least I didn't feel like I had time to learn. I needed to slow down my life. I was in luck because the hit records stopped coming and my career did it for me.

The Bible says that there comes a time when we should put away childish things and go on to bigger and better things. I had to put away the childish things.

Even if you look at many of the great biblical figures, like Solomon—the richest, most powerful man in the world during his life—there always came a point at which they had to make a serious change in their lives and stop living immaturely. Solomon literally read every book there was. After all that he came to the point where he realized that all his "seeking" had been in vain. In a way I came to the same point. I am not comparing myself with Solomon, but the biblical lesson was clear. I had been so successful and I had shared my music with the world, but I had to repent. To me, "repent" simply means stop, turn around, think, and go in a different direction.

At my "mess" point life was kicking me in my butt. So was my "mess" all bad? If life weren't like that, I might not be here to teach something at an older age.

HAVE YOUR BUCKETS READY

One of the first steps in my new walk was to stop blaming others for my problems. There was a point in my life when I blamed Russell for anything in my career that I couldn't control. I said that all along it was me out on stage "tap-dancing" while he had been "Mr. Businessman"— behind the scenes, starting and running Def Jam Records, and becoming the biggest mogul in the history of hip-hop. When I hit on hard times, I felt it was time for him to give something back to me. When I felt that way, I was in a place where I looked up and said, "I didn't start any groups. I didn't open a label. I didn't do anything. I was busy trying to be a star. And there was money to be made in being a star. But there's a lot of money in this—I mean you guys are rich now." It's like I was saying, "You owe me. I gave you the fuel to drive that car so that you could make that trip. I feel like you guys are doing great—but every article says that Run helped you."

But I have grown since then.

There's absolutely no animosity about this today, and Russell and Lyor Cohen, Russell's business partner, agree that while I may not have "made" the money for them, I was a spark to get everything going. And now we work together on all kinds of projects. For example, I am the head of Def Gospel, which has a whole line of artists in the works. But, like when I started out rapping, it will take a lot of work to build that label. And whether it works or not, I will take full responsibility and blame or credit for my role.

I tell you this story now because I want this book to reflect the truth. There was a point when I felt like, "You guys have become a big corporation with this rap thing and I lost focus, because I felt like I was just rapping. Wow. I can't believe that now. We all have our roles."

What I didn't realize at that time was that you should never be angry at someone else's success. Russell loves me and always has, and precisely because we are honest with each other about how we feel, nothing can come between us. The reality in the way the universe operates is that there's more than enough success and prosperity and opportunity to go around for everybody. Success is like sunlight. You don't have to hoard it, and really you can't. We all can shine. When you basically take responsibility for yourself, that's when you can get ready to move to the next level. You make a big mistake when you don't expect abundance from the universe. When abundance comes for some people, they're either in disbelief, too shocked to be ready, or too blind to see what they've been asking for in their prayers. We all need to have great expectations for and of ourselves to make our transformations complete. You have to get your buckets ready to catch the bounty you will receive when you learn to expect abundance. What good is it if God opens up the windows of heaven and you don't have your buckets ready to receive your blessings?

A lot of people blame the world. They say, "The black man can't get a job," or, "The world is mean to me because I'm a woman," or, "I can't get ahead—everybody's jerking me." But you know what? It's the inner strength that makes the difference. When people feel like someone else is holding them back from what they should really be getting, doing, and having, I say to them, "Whatever you want to have you have." Don't blame anybody for you not having success at this point in your life. You have the same chance as everyone else. We're all in this race together. You have the same resources to pound the pavement. Get your self-help books; make your connections. There was this guy who liked giving parties. He would put fliers up all over Queens and Manhattan. He then met a man with a special gift. And, well, the two got together and started throwing parties. One would rap, and the other would arrange the show. Well, this young entrepreneur began to grow large and took the next step and created his own record label. He became rich. He eventually made millions. Sound familiar? Russell Simmons and Def Jam. There was another young man who had a dream of becoming a rap star. Sound familiar?

You can do this—anybody can do this. Anybody—black, white, yellow, green, blue, or purple. Nothing is holding you back.

"Nature abhors a vacuum," or the universe tries to fill every available space. But the problem that we have is often we don't make space for God to give us anything new, all the while complaining about how we don't have what we want and need.

Having your buckets ready means opening yourself up to receive all the good that God has in store for you. But you can't do it if you're still holding onto unnecessary things from the past. If your hands are tied holding buckets full of things you don't want, how can God give you the things that you do want? How can God give you buckets of diamonds if you don't have any room? If my table is covered with old things, how do I have room for anything new?

Any time you make a decision in life, as one door closes, another opens up. Life is always like this. You can't be afraid of not having what you want.

A Personal Transformation

I was afraid when I walked into Zoe Ministries that first Sunday morning, but I knew I had to be there. I first heard about the ministry from one of Run-D.M.C.'s bodyguards. I saw its television broadcast and decided I would pay Zoe a visit. After that first day, I started going on a regular basis. I became obedient, humble, and dedicated to the church. No task at the church was beneath me. One day I would do Bible study work. The next I'd be working with the television ministry. One day I seated a teenager and his grandmother who had come to church together. The kid was just staring at me. I overheard him saying, "Grandma, that usher over there is Run-D.M.C.!" His grandmother said, "Shut up! All you think about is that rap music. Run-D.M.C. ain't no usher in a church!" Things like this happened all the time, and people who knew about it in hip-hop started making fun of me. But still most of the hip-hop world didn't know that I was now carrying a Bible with me everywhere I went.

I had stopped smoking weed and started again. But after three or four months I didn't have the urge anymore. Zoe was really making a change in my life. A year and a half later I was a deacon and was as zealous in my duties as ever. Not too long after that Bishop Jordan made me "Reverend Run."

CHANGE IS GOOD

Slowly but surely my life started to change for the better. While I was sifting everything out I just completely dropped off the face of the earth for a year. No one really knew where I was or what happened to me during that time. While I was underground I was working on turning my life around. I saw what was wrong in my life as God's way of helping to guide me.

QUIET THINGS DOWN

It is hard to think when there is a lot of commotion, so I had to quiet things down, take time out for myself. Call it meditation, prayer, or therapy, quiet time is anything that helps you put the focus squarely back on you. You can do it anywhere—on your knees, in a hot sauna, on a baseball diamond or a running track. It's when you close out the world's distractions, allowing your mind to drift toward the center, where you can assess your needs, plan strategies, create discoveries, and resolve nagging issues that separate you from joy and happiness.

The day you begin putting the focus back on you is the day you will start seeing remarkable changes in all areas of your life. That's when you find your diamond and all the dirt around it disappears.

Calm down during the day. Plan. Take time to reflect. It's hard for people to reflect and think because they are so caught up in their hectic schedules and don't take time to plan and organize.

There's a mind-set that successful people get. The second you can create that type of flow is when you'll start achieving success. You have to begin to hear and feel all aspects of your life. You've got to constantly take stock of your thoughts and analyze why and how things happen to you.

FORGET ABOUT LUCK

Taking control of your mind means you have to banish the belief in luck. Like one famous golfer said, "Golf is a game of luck. The more I practice, the luckier I get." Luck is a crutch that unsuccessful people use as an excuse for their failures. Some people believe that things just happen to certain people. But I find great things happen to people who expect to be blessed.

Self-awareness is the key to life. And living from within should be everybody's top priority. If you were brought up to believe in luck, your brain might tell you otherwise. But until you reject those old, dependent ways of thinking and accept the truth of yourself, you'll never be at peace with the world.

No one ever has to settle for less than the best, but only ignorance will limit you. Until you accept that you are an expression of God and that He lives in you, you will stay stuck. His power is limitless, and since you are an expression of God, yours is, too.

I CHANGED MY MIND

All things begin from within.

Ideas create our world, and your thoughts determine your state of

If that ain't an old school pose, tell me what is.

It's funny, everybody L. L. ever battled got their butt kicked real bad. Poor Kool Moe Dee and Canibus. Some people never learn.

Jay's philosophy on how to rip the spot tonight.

On tour with the Beasties holding it down night after night.

Louder, Dee, louder!

Good old days. Check out my walk.

The first crossover rock-rap joint, this changed history.

Dee doing the King of Rock.

Right here I'm saying, "Let's do this!"

There's vintage Run ripping the spot down.

Show's over. Peace out, everybody!

My homies Jay, Dee, and Runny Ray.

The Eiffel Tower. I remember that like yesterday. . .walking down the block
laughing, and then a dude said, take a picture right here.

consciousness. When a person isn't happy inside, nothing in life will ever bring him any joy. Your spirit is the source of your experience, and until you examine your mind you'll forever be in bondage. When you don't nurture your spirit, your conscious mind will always keep divine light from ever entering your world. You'll compromise your infinite potential and never achieve what you're looking for.

Opening the world of possibilities that's within you requires commitment and patience. To change your life, you must first change your mind. You have to work hard to master your thoughts. You can learn to control your thinking and regulate your will. An undisciplined mind creates confusion. And as I can truly attest, confusion ultimately leads to upset.

To ward off disaster and danger, you have to identify old habits, spot patterns, and begin cutting away that conditioning that has built up over the years, clogging your spirit with false ideas about what is and what isn't important for your well-being. Some people will live in hell, not heaven, simply because they don't know any better. They'll wallow in pity and self-doubt. To some people, life will always be wrapped in mystery and nothing will ever seem to make sense. A lot of people don't even want answers—they'd rather live in ignorance. You are the sum of all your thoughts, and if you don't like you, change your mind and move on. If a person wants to be happy and healthy, he must think happy, healthy, and abundant thoughts and not limit himself. I was finally happy, healthy, and loving myself. The blessings were coming in abundance.

I had taken my light back.

RUN'S HOUSE RULE

No. 7

You Can Stage a Comeback!

Problems occur to help direct you in life. Sometimes we only learn the value of something by losing it. Never believe it is over. I lost everything. My self-esteem was low, my vision clouded. But, deep inside, I knew that if I hung in there long enough and kept the faith I could make a comeback.

If your life isn't what you think it should be, don't give up. This book is living proof that you can stage a comeback.

It's Like This . . .

- God is into the details.
- To repent means to stop, turn around, think, and then go in a different direction.
- You should never be angry at someone else's success. Success is like sunlight: there's more than enough to go around, and you can't hoard it.
- Make God a promise not to forget Him.
- Make yourself a promise that you will take the quiet time to find out what really matters in your life.

THE WORD: "Likewise the Spirit also helpeth our infirmities: for we know not what we should pray for as we ought: but the Spirit itself maketh intercession for us with groanings which cannot be uttered."

—ROMANS 8:26

REVEREND RUN: "...I realized what a terrible mess I had made of my life.... I was at the absolutely lowest point in my life. It was then that I knew God was listening and my life was headed for a change.... My first move was to deal with my issues of denial. I wasn't being honest with myself and how I had been living."

EXERCISE

Say to Yourself

"Where my attention goes, my mind power flows. I am a creative force, and every day I am going to quiet my mind so that I can be divinely inspired and used by God."

Make a quiet time for yourself every day. Figure out what time works for you. For me, my quiet time is definitely at night. It's when all my creative inspirations have struck. There would be nights when my family would all be asleep and I'd go down to the basement, put on some records, and be creative. Sometimes I'd listen to a Prince record or other types of records and through the process I'd bring it up to a rap level. Like once I was listening to "Mickey" by Toni Basil and it inspired me to write the hit "It's Tricky." "Raspberry Beret" inspired me to write "You Be Illin'." And believe me, this was the most creative thing, because this was way before people had even thought of sampling. When you get all the chaos in your life out of the way, you can put everything in perspective and let the creative spirit flow through you.

8

GIVING: A FORMULA FOR SPIRITUAL SUCCESS

The Lord is my light and my salvation; whom shall I fear?
The Lord is the strength of my life; of whom shall I be afraid?
—Psalms 27:1

IT WAS THREE DAYS before Christmas and I had about a thousand dollars to my name, the millions spent and gone. This was not too long after the dismissal of the rape case, which cost me hundreds of thousands of dollars to defend. These were difficult times for sure. My family had grown to depend on me, and like any man, I liked having them depend on me. I had always produced, but this time something was different. I was nervous. Maybe the well had run dry.

I had gotten very used to spending big and living well. I always was a cheerful giver, sharing my wealth with others, buying some close friends cars, and helping others out financially. But now that I was poorer there was only enough to buy a Christmas tree and a few presents for my wife and children, not to mention the rest of the family. Still, I was going to church regularly, trying to do all the right things to maintain my spirit and protect my soul, including tithing.

My initial attitude about going to church was "I'm over." I was spent. I knew I needed to be there, but I also wanted to continue to give to the Lord because He had given so much to me. But I was close to being broke. And when you have had hundreds of thousands of dollars, having only a thousand dollars can be hard to digest. What was I gonna do? My instincts told me, *I'm sick; I need a doctor.* So I went looking for a prophet. If you got ill right now, your family would suggest you go see a doctor. But I knew my sickness wasn't physical but spiritual. At least I was smart enough to finally say, "This is crazy; I need *God.*" This time I was at an emotional crossroads, but I didn't turn to alcohol, other drugs, or women. No. This time I went to see Bishop Jordan.

Every week Bishop Jordan was prophesying to me. And he was helping me to turn my life around. And every week he wanted money! That's all he talked about. He showed me Scriptures from the Bible. He would tell me the story of the prophet Elijah and how an old lady was sitting about to eat her last meal with her son when Elijah came into town. God sent him because God had dried up the nearby brook. Everybody wondered why God would send the prophet to a broke old lady, but the prophet approached the old lady and demanded, "Give me your last meal." She said, "This is the last pancake in the house. My son and I were going to eat it and then die." The prophet said, "Give it to me and you and your family will eat forever." The son was sitting there shivering and hungry. The mother said, "It probably will kill us, but my faith says give the food to the prophet—the man of God." So she cut the pancake and poured the syrup, and the prophet ate it. The next thing you know, sure enough, they ate for the rest of their days. Now, Bishop Jordan tells the story much better and a little different, but this is how I remember it. The woman could have easily refused—she and her child were starving, after all—but she somehow found it in her heart to just trust. She let go of what she had, and, amazingly, she and her son ended up with more than she dreamed.

The bishop read this story from the Bible and asked, "Do you believe the Bible? I'm the prophet. You guys are broke. Give me your last and you will eat for the rest of your days."

From the day I first set foot in Zoe, the bishop had been stressing the importance of planting seeds. He touched on that topic again one Sunday before Christmas, and then he turned the pulpit over to a minister from another church. The visiting minister's sermon about gratitude had everyone magnetized, and he ended it by coaxing us to empty our pockets—in other words, give the biggest possible offerings. When he said that my mind started to spin. I had to check myself.

When I first went to church I was a skeptic. I didn't know what to think at first. Having grown up in the streets of Hollis, Queens, and being in the music business, I was used to people running games and scamming everybody. Hearing this (as far as I was concerned) greedy so-called prophet talking about "gimme your money," I had to be skeptical. I thought about Daddy Rich, the jerk artist-preacher in the *Car Wash* movie. That's all I knew. I thought, *This guy is gonna jerk me.* I didn't know anything about Zoe Ministries. I was just some b-boy cat who was depressed and broke. But at the same time I was thinking, *I've got no other choices. I've got to believe in something.*

I looked at the bishop and thought to myself, *This guy is rich already. This church looks great. What does he need my money for?* But I'm there and the visiting prophet is saying, "Give him money." My first wife had left several years earlier, and my new wife, Justine, and I are sitting there with the kids together in church. I've got a normal household now. I'm not doing that well, but I'm still following God. The prophet is preaching to the whole church that we should give our last. But I'm wondering, *Should I? I owe all this stuff. I'm getting myself together, and I have a little bit of money in my pocket, but I'm basically just surviving from week to week. I've got money, but I don't even have enough for a "real Christmas."*

I'm sitting there wondering, *Do I believe this?* I'm battling with myself internally over giving this last money. Finally I put the money in the basket and I go on home. I just hope that God will work it out. Now I don't have *any* money and Christmas is still coming.

I go home and just start sitting in the tub and meditating. But I was still fighting the prophet because I only had two days before Christmas for God to work—as if God can't work in one second! I'm concerned, but I turn it over to God. I let it go and had faith that I'd be provided for. I finally released my seed because it couldn't meet my need, and the next day I ran into my harvest. Monday I called my accountant and he said, "It's funny you should call; we just got a check here from some old royalties." He sent me the check, and it was more than enough to take care of Christmas and a good time into the future.

I already knew the principles of giving and receiving because by that time I had been going to church for a while, but the big question in my mind was *Do I dare to believe again?* Was the royalty check a sign? My financial problems were more strenuous than usual. Now bills were piling up. But I dared to believe again. It's an ongoing belief that says, *Let go and let God.* Supply the prophet. Feed that prophet. And believe that God is going to release a blessing in your hand because you released it and released your fear.

The key is, if an amount of money isn't enough to meet your need anyway, it's only a seed. This thousand dollars was not going to meet my need, so I knew in my heart it was only a seed. Now, I know a thousand dollars is a lot of money for most people, including me, but at the time I needed more, thousands more, to be my personal payroll. But I had no safety net. My trust was purely in God and the universal principles: Give and it shall be given. Let go and let circulate. Let your faith go and know that God will take care of you like He takes care of the birds of the air. Let go and know that the universe is always supplying air. Let go and know that the oceans are always here for water. Let go and know that when you plant a seed in the ground, fruit will grow.

When I first started going to church, things didn't get better right away. I still felt I had nothing to live for. But I just kept going anyway. I kept going. I kept giving. I kept hearing the Scriptures. The bishop kept showing me these stories about the science of how the mind works. He said that sometimes it's the prophet's job to take your last in order that you shall eat the rest of your days.

Christmas had always been important to me, a really big deal. I must admit when I put the money in the basket that Sunday I was thinking I could just go pick up a small tree, maybe a few gifts, buy dinner, and my family would be straight. But I knew that in order to satisfy both God and me this time I had to have more faith than I ever had before. I had to change my behavior for a different result. I took the walk into faith.

When I decided to give the money I was holding in my pocket to the prophet, I stepped to the front of the church and knelt before the altar to receive my blessing. I still had no idea how my family was going to make it through the holidays, but somehow I knew we would prevail. I had total confidence in what was to come.

There are amazing stories of faith throughout the Bible. We can draw inspiration from all of them. But one of my favorite stories is told by Reverend Ike about a thirsty man and a rusty pump. The man approaches the pump and sees a glass of water with a note instructing him to prime the machine with the liquid. He could opt to lubricate his throat instead, satisfying his immediate desire, but if the priming process worked he would have buckets of water for years to come. He decided to pour the water, and, miraculously, a big stream soon started to gush forth.

Am I saying that you should give your last? I can't tell you what to do, but I can say that giving releases the faith that you believe more will come. It doesn't have the mentality of "I will never get again." You don't walk around saying, "I have five dollars. And if I don't save and hoard this five dollars I will never have five dollars again." Or, "I won't have it when I need it." Release it so you can release your clogged mind—and stop believing in *scarcity.*

Giving in times of famine can test your faith like nothing else can. It is an all-out acknowledgment of one's humanity, and doing it consistently with a happy heart will greatly advance any spiritual journey.

Through practice we all can learn the importance of never becoming attached to things. We can witness the benefits of generosity while experiencing all the wonderful feelings setting things free can bring.

Like all actions in the physical world, giving begins from within. It's an act of love, so in order for you to become a cheerful giver, you first have to feel whole on the inside. If you don't, you can never be truly generous to anyone.

PURE GIVING

Giving rightly is about purity of intention. Any time you get to the purity of yourself in any respect, you are fulfilling your purpose, forging your own unique path. Instead of walking through life as though a carrot is constantly dangling in front of your face, you become less calculating and attached to an outcome. You perform simply for the love of it. You give yourself to any task without regard for what you might get back. And whenever you serve with all your heart you get a present; the universe always rewards you. That's the coolest thing about this life.

The same thing happens for an athlete. Our most beloved sports stars are the ones who don't hear cash register bells every time they hit a home run or sink a basket. We see purity in their pursuits and beauty in their moves. Watching Michael Jordan run the boards was watching a man who would have been happy just to have a basketball in his palms. Since he stepped into the NBA, fans flocked to the arena to see him game after game, event after event, because they detected *purity* in what he was doing. He gave the game everything he had, and people happily, respectfully, nominated him for superstardom.

Recording artists who create music from their hearts instead of their heads will strike a bigger chord in the marketplace than all the fakers out there. Hearing Lauryn Hill's album and D'Angelo's album and R. Kelly, you can tell they were creating their music with the right spirit.

Take Cree Summer, for example, the actress who played a ditzy coed on the sitcom *A Different World*. She always wanted to sing. She was in a black rock band, called Subject to Change, which used to gig all up and down the Sunset Strip in LA. The group eventually got signed to a major label, and on the very day its album was due to drop they were cut from the label. I don't know all the reasons why, but they were dropped. This was heartbreaking for Cree. She'd been actively chasing her dream of becoming a recording artist for years. Then it all crumbled.

At first she shunned everything related to music. She stopped listening to the radio, playing CDs, and writing songs. Then she came to the revelation that art is still art if no one sees it or hears it. She started pouring her soul into creating her kind of music again, what she was hearing in her heart. With no thoughts of landing a record deal, she gave a tape of her new material to her best friend and soul sister, actress Lisa Bonet, who passed it on to her now ex-husband, Lenny Kravitz. He and Cree had not seen each other in more than a decade, but he heard the tape and jumped at the opportunity to work with her.

Assisted by his clout in the record industry, Cree landed a contract with a new, more caring label. Now she's out touring and touching people all over again. All because she gave with the right spirit.

Multitudes are incapable of giving freely. These are folks who can be counted on to always find fault or complain. They only look at the dark side, and nothing is ever quite right for them. No one is ever good enough, either. Their focus stays squarely on what is wrong, and they will sulk and brood over the things the next man has, feeling that life has somehow robbed or cheated them out of owning these things, too. Never quite grateful or appreciative, they can stand in front of a roomful of friends and family gathered in their honor and still feel unloved. "No one cares for me!"; "No one likes me!"; and "Everybody hates me!" are some of their favorite whines. Clearly, their perspective is all screwed up.

Do ten things right for them, they'll search for that one thing that's wrong. Hand them a surprise gift and they will grudgingly accept it, all the while wishing it were something else. Something bigger. Something more. When you can't give, you can't receive, either—even when God is *trying* to give to you. These kinds of people become angry and keep those feelings bottled up inside until they explode without warning. They ignore everything around them, which keeps them from ever having the happiness that they want. They always feel like they're alone. They're never connected to the rest of the world and the universe. Their whole life becomes empty because they are never thankful for anything.

Everything in our world—from a song to a bright painting—is a gift of one kind or another. When you get all pessimistic and ignore the beauty around you, you end up with a hole in your soul. Then you start belittling what you want that you don't have. That just drives it further away from you. You're just cutting yourself off from all the possibilities in life. Everyone wants to break into fresh new areas of life, but some people constantly complain and don't appreciate what they already have, so that they can never get any more.

GIVING ENERGY

I have experienced lots of days when I felt down, riding a heartbreak or nursing a disappointment. During these times I tend to appreciate all the gifts in the world—I count my blessings: my wonderful wife, Justine; my five beautiful children, Vanessa, Angela, JoJo, Daniel, and Russell; and my health. Everything is a blessing when you think about it. Whoever you are, God has given you a lot. Nothing knocks me off my feet better than a bright sun or a bird chirping. These are a few of the abundant miracles of life that we forget.

Too often we don't pay respect to the contributions fellow human beings make to our lives. We dismiss their praises or ignore them alto-gether. This is a fast-paced society where everyone rushes. Or they feel they must be hard to avoid being labeled soft or a pushover, especially in hip-hop music. These are attitudes of ungratefulness, which dull our God-given shine. Showing kindness to people can help you mani-fest the greatness in your life.

There's this guy who always hangs out on the avenue near my house. He washes the windows of all the passing cars. Whenever I drive by I try to toss him a dollar or some loose change. I don't judge him. I don't question what he's going to spend it on. I just try to acknowledge his efforts. Just like me, he is a person of God, and just like the reflections of myself that I see in nature, he brings me joy.

One morning I wasn't feeling too good when I came to the corner he hangs on. I was digging in my pocket and shuffling through the ash-tray, but I kept coming up empty. He saw me going crazy, and he just looked in, smiled, and said, "Nothing today." Not a question — just a statement. That made me feel good, and it changed the course of my day. I told him, "Thank you!" Just like he always tells me. I think that in that instant the good feeling that we were giving each other every day wasn't really about the money at all.

Every time we come into contact with another person, energy is exchanged. If, for example, you ran into a jealous, miserable person on the day you closed the biggest deal of your career, instead of being elated, you might be brought down to the level of the other person.

BECOME A GIVING GIVER

To open things up so you can start becoming a giving giver, you have to stop taking people and things for granted. You have to stop looking at yourself as a victim and start recognizing all the things you have. You have to have a heart of compassion and be willing to give to people who don't have what you have. And I'm not just talking about money. The best thing that you can give is part of yourself—your time, your energy, your love.

Most of us have heard the story about the man who felt so bad because he had no shoes until he was strolling down the street and saw a man with *no feet*. He saw how different his own life would be if he were an amputee and suddenly appreciated his place. In gratitude you will begin to move away from a lonely point of lack to a more enlightened place of richness and abundance. Gratitude allows you to forge new paths toward getting all the things you'll ever want.

Take the case of a young person who enters the workplace cold, not knowing anybody and having nothing but dreams and ambition. As she begins to network, attempting to move closer and closer toward fulfilling her purpose, she'll encounter many people who will assist her on this journey. Along the way, someone may give up a tip about an available position or offer a name she can use to open a few new doors. She makes a mistake if she just takes the info and runs without looking back. If you live life like that, eventually all the connections will dry up, because everybody will know that you're stingy and you only think about yourself.

See, giving and receiving are how everything in the world works. All acts and actions are part of this scheme where one thing is exchanged for another. Something gives; something receives. Life and death. A big fish might eat a smaller fish but in turn will be caught by a fisherman and become part of a balanced meal that nourishes several human beings.

A leaf that falls off a tree doesn't simply go to waste, either. It will descend to earth, decompose, and become fertilizer, which will feed that same tree as well as others around it, causing them to bear fruit and even more leaves.

Trees always know their leaves will grow back. So when fall comes, they gladly shed them. Humans, however, with all our fears, will not let go of things, then say, "Ugh, I want my stuff back! . . . Where are my leaves going? . . . Why is my wardrobe leaving? . . . Why are the wheels going the wrong way?"

These feelings come from ignorance, not knowing that almighty God, who created the universe, works far better for you than He ever could for a tree. Trees don't have a mind, so they don't care about the changes. We do have a mind, so we get scared and worried. We want to glue our leaves on, not knowing that there's a season to shed and a cycle is at work.

Hoarding or being stingy interferes with the natural flow of things. It comes from a consciousness of lack and the mind-set that there is not enough to go around, which creates a resistance to giving. Your thoughts create your world; feelings of lack will keep you always in need, never satisfied, always unfulfilled.

Breathing is yet another manifestation of giving and receiving. For every breath you take, you have to give one back. When you breathe in oxygen, you breathe out carbon dioxide, which is food for the plants that give up the oxygen we need to live.

INVEST IN YOURSELF

The process of giving and receiving works the same way in the spiritual realm as it does in the physical plane. When you let go of hatred, you get back many times the kindness. If you want love, you have to give love. If you want recognition, you're going to have to give props to other people. If you want money, you're going to have to invest in yourself.

A few summers ago, Reverend Ike told me a story about sailing across Europe. Because the upper portion of the vessel was packed with people, he decided to go to the lounge, which was less crowded. He saw people casually sipping drinks and chatting while being entertained by a tuxedo-clad piano player who seemed to be about twenty-five. His sound was sweet and seductive, and it seemed to pull people closer to him. Reverend Ike said he approached the man and noticed an empty oversize martini glass sitting atop the piano. Always the instigator, the reverend stuck his head in the musician's face and inquired, "Is that container for drinking or for money?" He knew the answer, and the man confirmed that it was for money. Reverend Ike replied, "Well, why is no money in it?"

The piano player shrugged his shoulders. "I don't know," he said. And he continued playing.

With a knowing look, the Reverend reached into his pants pocket for his wallet. He pulled out a crisp hundred-dollar bill, tossed it in the glass, and walked off. When he came back the glass was overflowing with money. The piano player couldn't figure out what had happened.

The following day Reverend Ike returned to the lounge. When he looked into the glass, all he saw was a single dollar bill. And for the next few minutes there were no new offerings.

"What happened to the hundred-dollar bill?" Reverend Ike asked. The piano player shrugged. "Take that dollar outta there and put the hundred back," Ike said. Reverend Ike went around the boat and did his thing, and nature took care of business. Once more, like before, when the reverend returned he saw the glass overflowing with money. Finally, Ike explained to the piano player that he cannot expect anybody to give to him until he gives to himself.

Giving doesn't have to be limited to handing out dead presidents. You can give of your time. You can share your knowledge and experience. Lend a helpful hand or maybe a caring ear. You see, giving to yourself is the ultimate acknowledgment of the forces within us. It's a full appreciation of who we are and what we have to offer the world. When we thank people, we demonstrate love for ourselves. Our hearts radiate these warm feelings outward, and because nothing attracts anything better than itself, the world responds in kind. A gift basket, an offer to pay for lunch, or even a thank-you note can do a lot to nurture a relationship. The effect of gratitude is support.

SEED TIME AND HARVEST

We have all no doubt heard the phrase, "It is better to give than to receive." But in actuality, like I said, the two are equal, one and the same—like joy and pain. They form a basic law of nature—the basis upon which the whole world runs. As the planets spin, it is quite clear that practically every process we can imagine involves the acts of giving and receiving.

Run-D.M.C. have always been givers. When we first came out, rap wasn't mainstream, yet we got prime-time play all over. It was an East Coast thing, with only a handful of artists, like Grandmaster Flash and the Furious Five and Kurtis Blow, able to play stadiums and arenas as opening acts. So we performed lots of free shows in the Midwest, out west, and down south, which broke through doors and blazed a trail for others to follow. We gave our music with love and planted seeds that were the foundation for our success.

We also lovingly created the blueprint for new forms within the hip-hop art form. Our rock-rap fusion, which got exposure on such jams as "Rock Box" and "Walk This Way," prepared the world for groups like the Beastie Boys and Korn. These musicians and others give us the utmost respect, which enables us to not only maintain in the game all these years but also prosper in it, getting shows and press even when we don't have a record out.

Though we weren't preachy, Run-D.M.C. also gave listeners words of inspiration through our music. We prided ourselves on always staying positive. In "King of Rock," after we dropped the line "*Run goes to school every day,*" kids used to come up to me all the time telling me that I kept them going to school when they felt lost and were ready to drop out. Other people told me that they'd play a Run record whenever they were sad and then they'd feel better.

Of course we contributed to lots of charities. The album we did for the Special Olympics, *Christmas in Hollis*, sells every year, and the set we played for Live Aid so inspired us that we were compelled to write about it in our song "My Adidas." For Run-D.M.C. giving has always been important, because we still remember what it was like when we were trying to make it. I think the *Christmas in Hollis* album sells very well every year because people know that it is about giving something back, giving something of yourself during a special time of year. The CD is sincere, coming from the heart. What I once took for granted I don't anymore. The CD is pure and innocent.

When we released *Raising Hell* we received our harvest. By doing all those unpaid gigs in '83, '84, and '85, we were planting seeds. To create a better life for yourself, you have to let go of unhealthy things. If a person believes nothing is missing in his life, he won't dwell on what he doesn't have. "That's all I have" is the absolute worst state of consciousness. That's a lack of consciousness. If you get into a place where you believe, *I'm never gonna get any more*, you never *will* get any more. If you can believe that money is like air, which is always here, you'll know it's always available. You'll know more will come to you. But if you keep thinking it's scarce—that there's only this little bit and that you'll never see any more—you'll never get anything because you believe there's not enough. That's a terrible consciousness, and I don't live that way. There's always more than enough for me. I think of myself as a tree—always being replenished according to the laws of the universe.

Yesterday's home runs don't win today's games, so it is always time to step up to the plate and swing the bat again. And again. And again.

WHAT TO DO WHEN TIMES ARE HARD

When times are hard, it is pretty easy to find excuses for not giving. You could be looking at unpaid bills and seeing nothing but cutoff notices or staring at bare cupboards and seeing only famine. You might be thinking you have nothing left to offer yourself, much less others.

If you open up your heart, you'll be more appreciative of everything. Instead of focusing on what you do not have, you'll be thankful for the gifts you do have. Nothing will be taken for granted.

When things seem hopeless, it always helps to count your blessings. The bus operator's smile in the morning is a gift. A Saturday afternoon stroll in the park under cloudless blue skies is a gift. The song on the radio that suddenly invaded the brain fuzz and snatched your soul, that's a gift. A night spent chilling with friends, the sight and scent of a colorful floral arrangement, and even a torn and faded pair of jeans are gifts, too.

You can also give simple gifts to those around you. When you give your time without regard for what you'll get back, the reward is a natural high. That's the key to creating the sort of happy, peaceful life everyone craves.

The most valuable gifts aren't things you can buy. Think of how the Wright brothers must have felt the first time their airplane took off, defying gravity, after they had toiled day after day, experiencing one failure after another. They weren't motivated by money; they were driven by a deep passion, an unshakable belief in their ideas.

That diamond inside you is your particular gift. If you could describe yourself in one word, you're on the right course. If somebody mentions Run, you'll say, "rapper." If you can't sum up what you do without stuttering and stalling, then maybe you don't know what you're supposed to be doing. Maybe you're not giving the world what you came here to give it.

Giving is what gave Puff Daddy his edge. Before he blew up and became a major player, he put in hours in nightclubs, watching people and studying what made them move. He'd slip into spot after spot, studying the crowds like an eager student. Using the research, he and his studio squad, the Hitmen, went on to craft bouncy beat treats that delighted millions of listeners. And though he's been criticized for sampling too much, his use of loops (pieces of previously recorded music) is part of a continuum, a song cycle that grafts branches onto musical roots. He pays props (not to mention licensing fees) to veteran composers.

Puffy also gave lots of jobs to inner-city youth when he created his Bad Boy Entertainment company's street team, the first of its kind. He drew from its members' youthful energy and boulevard knowledge, which aided his all-out music industry assault.

Then there's my brother Russell. He gave birth to the entire rap music industry, for which he is still reaping the profits. When rap started, it was underground and an underdog. A whole lot of people didn't believe in its commercial potential. Not Russell. Now his company was just sold for $120 million. As his company, Def Jam, grew, he created opportunities for other entrepreneurs, like Puffy, Heavy D, and Andre Harrell. What all these people have in common is that they are winners because what they had to offer was right in tune with their purpose. They gave their gifts to the world, and the money just came.

See, everybody is sent to earth with a mission to do something. And when you figure out what it is and complete the mission correctly, with all your heart, then and only then will you be rewarded.

You never get money for doing what you're not supposed to be doing. Every time you're doing something that is beneficial not only to yourself but to everyone, you are contributing to society; you're giving of yourself. When money is not the only reason you're doing whatever you're doing, that's when you'll start getting paid.

Whenever you give with a joyous heart and you're happy to do it, things don't come back the same way. They come back with interest, multiplied many times over. A microscopic sperm and a microscopic egg create life—the most valuable gift of all.

And when you understand the law of giving and receiving, you'll understand how to save and invest. If you don't know the law, you might come into some money and blow it all, not knowing there will be a winter season coming soon. A farmer has to know when to go plant and when to sow, take what's needed, and replenish the earth. You can never take from something without giving back.

I used to give money and food to everybody. When I was rich it was easy for me to be generous, but when I was broke it was a whole different story. Giving is how you develop faith, because if you don't give—even your last—then you'll never really have the need to *test* your faith. All giving that is done with cheerfulness and comfort will result in many happy returns. Infect someone today with your powerful spirit of giving.

RUN'S HOUSE RULE

No. 8

Giving Is Receiving

You never get money for doing what you're not supposed to be doing. Every time you're doing something that is foul and not beneficial to yourself or others, nothing good can happen. There is no energy. But when you start living right, giving to others and contributing to society, then you are giving of yourself. The energy returns and the blessings flow.

It's Like This . . .

- If it's not going to meet your need, it's only a seed.
- Giving releases the faith that you believe more will come.
- Release your fear so you can unlock your clogged mind—and stop believing in *scarcity.*
- Giving in times of famine can test your faith like nothing else can.
- You cannot expect anybody to give to you until you give to yourself.
- You can never take from something without giving back.
- No one is so poor he has nothing to give, and no one is so rich he has nothing to receive.

THE WORD: "Every man according as he purposeth in his heart, so let him give; not grudgingly, or of necessity: for God loveth a cheerful giver."

—2 CORINTHIANS 9:7

REVEREND RUN: "The process of giving and receiving works the same way in the spiritual realm as it does in the physical plane. When you let go of hatred, you get back many times the kindness. If you want love, you have to give love. If you want recognition, you're going to have to give props to other people. If you want money, you're going to have to invest in yourself."

9

THE BIRTH OF REVEREND RUN

Lay not up for yourselves upon earth. . . . But lay up for your-
selves treasures in heaven.
—Matthew 6:19, 20

●NE DAY I was listening to New York City's Hot 97 and everybody was laughing about this new "Reverend Run." Everybody laughed about Reverend Run when I first became a minister. People were saying my being saved was a scam. People said, "This guy is ridiculous," that I had hit bottom and this was all a publicity stunt concocted to try to make a buck. People who I thought were my friends, who I thought would not only respect my decision but also be happy about it, were turning me into the laughingstock of the hip-hop world. I was the butt of jokes everywhere. But you can't listen to people. When God came into the center of my life, I just proclaimed it to the world and didn't care what people said about me.

That the Reverend Run was something they laughed at was painful, and I thought they would never stop laughing. But I also knew I was strong in my faith. I knew in my heart my beliefs were real and God was there with me. Still, I didn't blame people or take their remarks too personally, because I knew they didn't know any better. Who wouldn't laugh about a guy in this supposedly hard game of hip-hop music who would get in front of an audience with Ice Cube, Snoop Dog, Mac 10, and Puffy and call himself the Reverend Run? For me to come out and put on a clerical collar onstage and call myself the Reverend Run was the opposite of everything anybody knew. In a way, I would have been upset if I weren't ridiculed.

It was 1994 when I became a reverend, and gangster rap was on the top of the charts. Hip-hop music was all about being hard-core. I was used to the fact that whatever I stepped off into I was always looking foolish for a minute, so I felt comfortable in not following gangster rap, not following whatever was the flavor of the month, and instead doing something that seemed so ridiculous.

I like to be on the cutting edge. Standing out is hard. It's easy to go with a trail that's already been blazed, but being a pathfinder is a whole new thing, you've got to dig that dirt, and that's what I did, and everybody was able to follow me. That why I'm able to look back and say, "Been there, done that." That's why now, more than six years later, even the people who dissed me like crazy give me respect as both one of the founders of rap music and a man of the cloth. They realize that what I did by giving myself to God was something that I did for me and not for the world's approval. Now some of the very same people who wanted to laugh me off the stage back then call me when they need marriage counseling or want to get married or have a problem and don't know what to do.

Today I'm just blazing a new trail, only it's for the Lord.

And now I understand that it is never too late to turn things around. The "mess" I made of my life wasn't all bad, because now I have a whole new gift to give to people. If life were like that, crazy, I might not be here to teach something at an older age. Today I am just chilling trying to be myself, an obedient child of God. I mean imagine where I would be or what I would have become had things not slowed down for the character Run, the king of rap?

People often ask me if I would change anything about my life. I cannot say whether I would or not. If I had walked such a straight line, would I have been the same guy who made people happy? Would I have been Raunchy Run—that b-boy character that you *hoped* I was? Would I have been all those things I was that made me a big star to some of my fans? Would I have been that guy who created that culture that America loved? Would I have been that bold character who grew up in Hollis, Queens, where my environment taught me to be who I was and what I was? Was it good or wasn't it? I can't say that I would change it all. What I can say is that, looking at my life, I believe things are where they should be at this point. I'm right on course. I look at the world with no remorse and no sadness. I'm not behind in *anything*. I'm not behind in the rap game. I'm the Reverend Run and that is what I'm supposed to be doing at this point. I'm not behind because I would have never become the Reverend Run if I had continued at such a fierce pace. I would never have learned what was right and wrong and would never have turned my "mess into a message" if I had not sinned and fallen short of God. That doesn't mean you have to live a life of sin to be able to have God, just that we all have different paths to walk. And one's not better than the next, just different.

Try to get outside of yourself. What is "messy" about your life? Isn't it time you put certain things behind you? More important, what is God's message hidden in that mess that you've created? What are you living for? What is your mission? Find it! Find it and prosper.

BE FAITHFUL

Faith isn't something you say; it's something you do. You can't see it. You can't touch it. You can't read about it and then magically attain it. You can't even prove it's there. But you absolutely have to believe that there is a God-given treasure inside you, or you'll never be able to put forth the effort required to make it come out. Most people don't know what faith is. They think it's something you talk about. People tell one another, "You gotta have faith." But what we don't realize is that faith is nothing if it isn't in something. Your faith has to be in you and, more important, in God. Faith is the quiet knowing in your soul. It's not given; it's lived.

Faith is what gives you the power to do the *giving* that I talked about in the last chapter. I attribute all my good fortune to faith. I believe faith makes any incomplete life whole. And it was that faith in knowing God was with me when I was being talked about under the public microscope that allowed me to stand tall as Reverend Run. I could have backed off, but it was my strong belief and faith in my principles that let me know things would work out.

So many of us say we live by faith, but until we're truly tested we don't know what faith really means. Consistency is the key to unlocking faith in your life. When you are consistently faithful, you need not fear. Fear is just False Evidence Appearing Real, and it's the opposite of faith. With faith you can weather any storm.

If you let doubt and fear sleep with you, that's what you'll wake up with in the morning. But if you sleep with love, security, and happiness, then, like your favorite quilt, they'll keep you warm all night long.

It seems like a lot of the pivotal events in my life happen right around Christmas. This time it was just a few days before Christmas 1997 when my wife, Justine, and I learned the hard way that you have to keep faith in your inner treasure when it seems like everything in the world is telling you not to have faith. Our son Russell was only a couple of months old and hadn't been home that long when he started throwing up every day. We tried everything we could to help him get better, and nothing would work. He was getting skinnier and skinnier. It was about the seventeenth of December when we went to the doctor.

The doctor looked at Russell in a panic and said, "He hasn't gained weight in several months? We have to put him in the hospital!"

Christmas was coming. I wasn't going to get dumb and say, "No, don't admit him." But we were scared. I didn't want to get to heaven and say to God, "You never saved my baby!" and have God say, "I did show up; I was Dr. Bangeroo." (Yes, his name was really Dr. Bangeroo!) I didn't want God to say, "I showed up, but you were too caught up to recognize that I was using people to help you." So I let the baby go into the hospital.

They were running tests and Justine was bugging out while I was trying to find a way to remain calm. I kept repeating to myself, "It's all in God's hands." Hospital employees were putting different stuff up Russell's nose, giving him IVs, and taking blood, and he was going to have to spend the night. That night turned into days in the hospital. Then, just when I thought things couldn't get any worse, Justine called me frantically one day from the hospital saying, "Joey, oh my God, the baby can't breathe—he's turning blue."

I rushed to the hospital, and when I got there it was a scene of confusion. We had taken Russell to the hospital just because he was throwing up a lot, but now he couldn't even *breathe*. I started spending a lot of time praying with my prayer mother, Dr. Margaret Hannah. She told me that the baby would live and to hold onto my faith, but things were getting scarier and scarier. The hospital was killing him as far as I was concerned, and I started to feel that Russell didn't need to be there. I just wanted my son home. Justine and I didn't know when he was going to be able to come home, but we were just hoping that he would be released by Christmas, which was big to us.

The whole time we were in the hospital we saw babies going home with little machines to monitor their breathing, so that you'll know if they stop breathing in the middle of the night. Justine and I said to ourselves, *I'm so happy we don't have to take one of those things home.* But sure enough, our faith was about to be tested, because we were sent home with one of those machines. After all those tests, the doctors found out that Russell only had reflux and that he was going to be all right. Still, the machine had to go with us. That experience was a true test of our faith. It had seemed like everything was going great and I was getting my life on-track, and now this. I told Justine that everything was going to be OK, and my focus during that time was that I was not going to give this thing the utmost attention. I was not going to let this thing grow and keep growing because I was not going to give it *that* kind of audience. Justine was ready to cry. I believed it didn't matter and decided to take the machine, even though it looked scary. The machine made it look like Russell was on life support. Justine and I knew that he only had reflux, but he had to sleep with this thing. Every minute we were with him, he had all of these suction cups sticking on him. Sometimes the machine would go off in the middle of the night and scare us half to death, but thank God it was always a false alarm. It seemed to my family that Russell was really sick, like he was on the verge of death. But I knew that it was not a problem. The machine was only in case he stopped breathing when we were not around, and all that was wrong with him was reflux.

"Well, what happened? Why did he stop breathing at the hospital that day?" Justine asked. I didn't know, but I knew that Russell was going to be fine.

We got our first sign of encouragement when he came home the day before Christmas. But having this ugly metal machine with all these sounds and meters was killing Justine.

I said, "Let's not look at the machine like it's something bad; let's *love* it. Suppose he *does* stop breathing. It might help us. Why be pissed off at the machine?" I was kind of crazy, because every time Russell would even cough or something the machine went off. But after Justine and I started to treat the machine as our friend, Russell went off it a week later. Here's a time when we didn't give power to negativity. Russell could have been in the hospital for weeks, but it didn't happen. He was supposed to have this machine that we hated for a long time, but we didn't fight with it and it left.

In the end Russell was fine, and as I write this he is a happy, healthy two-year-old boy. But without faith we would have never made it through that ordeal. Whatever you fight you ignite. When situations come at you, don't get excited about them. When you get excited about them, they get excited about you. They start dancing for you. You give an audience a performance, and they're looking at you. The more you do, the more they give you cheers. Same thing with a situation. The situation comes for you to look at it. It wants to perform for you, but if you turn your head and don't give it that attention, it's not going to continue to dance. It's going to get tired of giving this performance, because you're not giving it an audience. So I didn't give that machine that kind of audience. That machine that was hooked up to Russell had no use in my home because it couldn't drive me crazy. And I took the fear out of my wife, so this particular performance of this machine in my home went off Broadway and then it went out of business.

Situations react according to the way you react to them. A situation can become frantic when you are frantic. Sometimes things can get so frantic when a bill comes that you can't pay. If you don't add negative energy to the situation, you can probably set the bill down, knowing that at some point the money will come to pay it. But no matter what happens, you can't pay the bill until you get the money.

When Run-D.M.C. is onstage we get more hyped as the crowd gets more hyped. Just the same way, the situation will get more hyped according to the way you're acting about it. Whether it's a utility bill or a sickness, it'll see that you are hectic and really want to get hectic *with* you. It's reacting and you're reacting, so now it's a whole big situation. It's there and you know it's there, but if you don't give it that type of energy it will dissipate and just leave.

This is the way I try to live my life. I try to give my attention to things that I want in my life. Whatever you give your attention to will tap-dance for you. If you give your attention to joy and happiness, then that will come out and tap-dance for you. Be aware of your consciousness. I think consciousness is everything. It's important to meditate, to sit quietly and see what's running around inside you. See what lies you can catch and get rid of. Discover what negativity is there that you can get rid of.

Don't Fall for Illusions

You've heard the phrase "keep it real." Well, I believed in not falling for illusions, so I did not entertain the thought that little Russell was sick. Staying strong in your faith lets you weather any storm. I forgot about the sickness. I knew in my heart that nothing would happen to the cute little guy and it was all going to work out, so I didn't fall for the illusion. My faith in the principles I learned was good.

I created my own reality through belief. For example, Magic Johnson created his own reality when he was told he had AIDS. He didn't let it worry him. He said, "I am coming through this," and his wife, Cookie, said he would be healed by Jesus. Next thing he's on the cover of *Ebony* magazine and *Black Enterprise*, saying, "I don't have a trace of AIDS." He's playing basketball, opening movie theaters nationwide, producing TV shows, and doing all kind of things. Who knows? Maybe he'll help discover a cure for this disease; you just never know, but my money is on him. Magic is still a winner. The important thing is that he didn't pay attention to what he was told he couldn't do with the disease; he didn't let it destroy him. Some people find out they have a sick child or a disease and their lives are destroyed. You have to have faith in yourself that things will work themselves out.

There's a story of a man inside a freezer. He gets locked in there and begins to shiver. He can't get out and gets colder and colder. He starts freezing to death. In the morning the door is opened and he is dead, lying there frozen, but the freezer was never plugged in! He believed that the freezer was going to kill him and *killed himself with fear*. You follow where I am coming from?

The mind is very powerful.

Another person could find himself in that same type of situation and keep saying to himself, "I'm going to live. I'm going to live." One day, someone will come along to rescue him. I saw a show about people who survive disasters, and the one thing they all had in common was that they all believed in their hearts that they were going to survive. People who die just give up belief that they are going to make it.

Faith Without Works Is Dead

People have faith in everything but God. Faith requires that you walk forward and do something for it to work. *Faith without works is dead.* The Bible says you can't please God without faith. You have to get up and go forward knowing that God is going to give you the breakthrough when you need it. Faith is going forward. If you're not going forward, then you don't have faith that something is going to work. Unfortunately, some people don't have that faith. For me, faith is believing a particular situation is going to happen. For me, my giving transforms into faith.

Your faith has to be *in* something. Faith isn't when you come up and say, "Have faith." What does "have faith" mean? I didn't just go to church and "have faith" that everything was going to be OK. I always have faith that God is going to help me in whatever way I need help that particular day.

Will Smith lives by faith; Russell Simmons lives by faith; Puffy lives by faith; I live by faith. Will Smith created a multimillion-dollar empire living by faith. Puffy created an empire and goes from Howard University back and forth to Harlem by stepping out on faith.

I imagine sitting under this big tree of bad luck that I have planted. The fruit from this tree hit me over the head every day. It's not fair. It's terrible. The world is crazy and I am getting exhausted, but I keep going forward planting the seeds of a new life, which I learned how to create at Zoe Ministries, a life based on consistent faith, or planting seeds for a new life. That's how you can create anything you want to have in your life. I planted those old seeds back then and waited before I reaped my harvest, a destructive life. So now I want to plant these new seeds, but it will take some time. Bad seeds are easy to plant. Good seeds are easy to plant. But both take time to come up. The harvest can be great, but you've got to be there to collect it. It's the time, the waiting, that kills you. That's why we need consistent faith. You have to continually believe that it will happen while waiting to harvest the seed. You have to be consistent even though it doesn't look like things are going to work out. Even when you may look crazy or strange to people. Know your faith.

When you have been eating less and working out for weeks and haven't lost a pound, do you doubt the laws of nature and the universe or does consistent faith keep you going? It will work if you let it. The definition of insanity is doing the same thing over and over and expecting a different result. If you do the same things every day, you should not be surprised when nothing changes. You have to break that pattern and start something new and go forward on that in order to get the new results. And when you get on a new path and you start to waver back to the old self, you need consistent faith to keep going.

What does faith mean? Faith is hope. It's knowing that something is going to happen. It's something you can't see in the physical world, but you know it's coming. You consistently believe what you want is going to happen for you, so you keep going. You know what a straight line is, and every day you walk it until you get to the place where you want to be. Consistent faith to me is continuing no matter what happens, against all odds, even though it looks like you are not coming out.

The result of consistency is that you are going to see results if you are on the right path. It's all about going in the *right* direction. If you're pointing in the wrong direction it doesn't matter how consistent your faith is. If you're pointing *west,* but you want to go *east,* you can have all the faith you want—you might get all the way to Arizona—but you'll never get *east.* When you're on the right path and doing the right thing, faith will get you anywhere you want to go. If you have consistent faith, you sit there like the cat at the mouse hole knowing that, sooner or later, dinner will be served!

No. 9

Have Faith!

You have to believe in yourself, period. You have to know that what you have is enough to get the job done. Don't be afraid. Know that you are the best and what you don't have you have the skills to get.

It's Like This . . .

- Whatever you fight, you ignite.
- Fear is the opposite of faith.
- Faith isn't something you say; it's something you do!
- Fear is just False Evidence Appearing Real.
- Situations react according to the way you react to them.
- Faith without works is dead.
- If you're pointing in the wrong direction, it doesn't matter how consistent your faith is; you'll never get where you want to go.
- Be like the cat at the mouse hole and know that what you desire is coming.
- Remember that if you are headed in the right direction good things will eventually happen. Consistency pays off.

THE WORD: "Therefore we are always confident, knowing that, whilst we are at home in the body, we are absent from the Lord."

—2 CORINTHIANS 5:7

REVEREND RUN: "Faith isn't something you say; it's something you do. You can't see it. You can't touch it. You can't read about it magically. You can't even prove it's there. But you absolutely have to believe that there is a God-given treasure inside you, or you'll never be able to put forth the effort required to make it come out. . . . Faith is the quiet knowing in your soul. It's not given; it's lived."

10

LIVE AN ENTHUSIASTIC LIFE

He restoreth my soul; he leadeth me in the paths of righteousness for his name's sake.

—Psalms 23:3

FAITH'S MOST IMPORTANT PARTNER is *enthusiasm*. If you drop the ball of enthusiasm, all the faith in the world will just fade away. If you can't be excited about something, you can't make it happen. Faith in your heart transforms into enthusiasm in your actions. The success of Run-D.M.C. has always been about the love and joy and enthusiasm we have for what we do. I now have the same enthusiasm about my ministry.

Enthusiasm is all about starting with what you have. You can never say, "I don't have what it takes," or, "I don't have what this person who grew up in Beverly Hills has to make it." Reading about Bill Cosby or Shaquille O'Neal or Whoopi Goldberg or anyone else who has made it despite starting out with what some could call nothing should make you realize that we all have something. We have the gifts that God gave us. Everybody isn't a great carpenter. We don't all have Michael Jordan's jump shot. But everybody has gifts. Once I sat on an airplane next to an older guy who was an orthodontist, and I was kind of surprised to find out just how much we had in common. But we couldn't trade places no matter how much either of us wanted. I couldn't go into his office and perform an operation on one of his patients' teeth, and he couldn't pick up a microphone and start rapping onstage. But it showed me how every person has something inside him that he really loves to do.

Where many people fall is by not knowing that their wealth is in their ideas and their talents. There's a book called *Do What You Love and the Money Will Follow*. What you love to do is where your true life is. But people spend their time doing things that they don't truly love. They do what they think they're *supposed* to be doing, but they don't enjoy their lives.

If you love something, make sure you would do it for free. Right now if I knew my friends were downstairs scratching and rapping in my basement, I would fight for the turntables. Even though I do it for tons of money, I would be standing over the turntables saying, "Give me the mike!" After a while, if you're not careful, you can actually put it into your mind that what you started out loving is some kind of *chore*. Sometimes I have to check myself on this. Now I get paid lots of money to do shows, and managers and stuff say, "Don't be late for this show" and, "Do your sound check!" I have put it in my mind at times that it's a chore. I have to remind myself that I'd be doing what I love no matter what. I know that I'm the boss in my life, and if I need a rest, I take it knowing that I'll wake up excited once again.

When I was getting my life in order I realized that my treasure, my diamond, was oration—the ability to speak—my gift of gab, so to speak. The same gift that made me a successful rapper is making me a successful minister. Rapping just became preaching. It's the same gift. When you find your gift, you'll get so enthusiastic about it that nothing will stop you. There comes a point when you say, "I'm leaving this job because I'm going for what I believe in." The bishop of my church once worked at the post office. One day enthusiasm rose up in him and he decided to leave to start a church with just five people. Now

not only does he speak, write books, and lecture, but he is also a millionaire and has been able to help scores of people turn their lives
around.

ENTHUSIASM AND MEETING PEOPLE WHERE THEY ARE

Enthusiasm is contagious, too. When you get excited, other people
can't help but catch your excitement. And you want them to. If I truly
feel I've been enlightened, it's my responsibility to share that with
everyone else.

This is a big part of my life, especially now, because I feel that that's
the way God approached me. With enthusiasm I give my absolute
best, and that feeling is like a universal language that everybody can
understand. When I do a concert, I don't wear my minister's collar out
onstage. Half the kids out there probably don't even have a clue that
I'm a minister. All they know is that I'm excited out there trying to rock
the mike. But still I'm able to reach them. Sometimes it's not about
wearing a sign on your forehead that says: "I'm a minister." Sometimes
you can speak better to people when they think you're the same person
they've come to know and love—in my case as a rapper.

When Sunday comes and I step into the church, I'm able to reach
a whole other set of people who would never have set foot at a rap concert. And I'm able to share with them the ways that God has been good
to me and the blessings He has put in my heart to share with the world.

When Jesus was alive, oftentimes when he spoke, different people
heard him in their different native tongues. And when he went to
speak to people, he was just as at home with the prostitutes and beggars
as he was with the nobility and the wealthy. He was able to minister to
them all according to their ability to listen. That to me is what godli-
ness is about—the pure excitement of feeling that makes me able to

speak the language that the people speak and able to reach people where they are.

If God weren't that way, He would've never been able to speak to me. At one point in my life, setting foot in any church was absolutely the furthest thing from my mind. If I had had to go to church to learn about the greatness that was inside me, I never would've learned. I try to always keep that in mind and remember that it's always going to be a case of "preaching to the choir" if the church members just get together with themselves week after week and year after year and reach out and never try to speak to a person who would have never set foot in the church. You have to go out there and expand. Fellowship and recruit others to share the Gospel, whether it's making a phone call to welcome someone new to town or passing on a Scripture or word of praise to the guy seated next to you on the airplane who is having a hard time. If you're not growing, you're dying. If a church isn't growing, it's dying. If you don't reach outside, you just dry up and die.

I am doing exactly what I am supposed to be doing at this point in my life, and I always have faith that things are going to work out. My life is exciting because I live in that secret place with God. His coming through gives me new ideas of all the ins and outs of every situation and keeps me on my toes. Being excited is always a miracle. Because of my faith, I see miracles constantly.

ENTHUSIASM GOES BOTH WAYS

Enthusiasm will color the whole way you see the world. It isn't necessarily good or bad. It's more like fuel for a car. It's what you need to get wherever you want to go. It's the feeling that makes you push forward when other people are giving up. It's easy to dwell on the ways that you can have great things by being enthusiastic about them. I can give you lots of examples of people who have used their enthusiastic spirit to succeed. But what people don't really think about is how enthusiasm about "negative" things can also bring them into being.

If you want to see exactly how negative enthusiasm impacts and shapes a person's life, look at the careers of Tupac Shakur and Biggie Smalls. Before being gunned down within months of each other, these rival rappers rhymed extensively about death and were obsessed with it. In magazine interviews and his records, Tupac talked constantly about death. He was spread out like Jesus on a crucifix on his last album cover. He used lyrics like, *"You're nobody until somebody kills you."* Biggie's first album was called *Ready to Die.*

People say, "Isn't it weird that they died?" But in a way, really, that's what they planned for. That's what they were enthusiastic about. They were *inspired* to write songs about it. They created album covers about it. It's always a challenge to live up to your divine nature. We don't recognize the power of thoughts and words. Look how many times we sell ourselves short by using our power of creation and visualization to create things that we don't really want. We have to keep reminding ourselves that our minds create our worlds. It's easy to forget sometimes because most people go around thinking that they can think whatever they want without ever having to face any consequences. But you constantly give birth to new things, whether fresh cells or some earth-shattering invention. Our minds can just as easily create good or evil. Our words make an impression on our subconscious. We all set ourselves up for our lives with our thoughts. And there's a fatal penalty for focusing your enthusiasm on the dark side. So I try to stay in the positive and allow my enthusiasm to carry me on, because I don't pretend to have all the answers, only the energy to search for them.

If You're Not Excited, Who Will Be?

Enthusiasm brings life to people. If you are enthusiastic about life, you're more likely to get what you want. You're going to be able to sell anybody on anything. You can feel the enthusiasm around a person in a room. When people see that you're enthusiastic, you are going to get the job done. They are going to get your feeling because of your enthusiasm. If you lack enthusiasm about something, how do you expect anybody else to be excited?

If I'm working on a project, when I step into the room anybody will tell you the look on my face is pure joy. I might start playing music and dancing around the room to it. I am enjoying it. I start making others get excited about it, too. You have to be enthusiastic about your dreams, because nobody will care about your dreams unless you keep your enthusiasm flowing.

You've got to be enthusiastic to run your business. To run it—to give it your soul from the beginning—you must be enthusiastic. Some people get fearful about leaving their nine-to-five jobs to follow their dreams. But some don't. Look at Keith Sweat. At one point he was making money working on Wall Street, but every evening he would go straight to the studio, meet up with Teddy Riley, and work on his record. Today he's a superstar R&B singer. If you love something, make sure you would do it for free . . . then do it enthusiastically. God made it so our talents would make us happy and more than sustain us. Your goal in life should be nourishing your youthful enthusiasm, which is so easy to lose if it gets beaten down every day. But when you have it, you wake up with a fresh new energy. You allow yourself to be used by God.

A lot of people fear that not having what they need stops them from ever starting anything. But the truth is that we all have a lot. When you start with what you have, you realize that you never have just a little. It may sound like I'm saying, "Even though you only have a little, start with the little bit that you do have and everything will be OK." But that's not what I'm saying. What I'm saying is that you actually have *abundance*. When you say "only," you put a limit on yourself: "I *only* have . . ." In life you're *full* of whatever God has given you. And He has given us all a lot. Start with what God gave you, and you'll see that you already have more than you need. See what you truly want, whether it's money, a new house, better health, or starting your own business. Don't worry; just relax your mind and know that God will always be there to sustain you.

RUN'S HOUSE RULE

No. 10

Start with What You Have—Enthusiasm

In order to generate success in your life you must bring the energy of enthusiasm. Enjoy who you are and what you bring to the table. Set your thoughts up so they are positive and you are in a position to capitalize on the opportunities for success your enthusiasm will create.

It's Like This . . .
- Whatever I become *fascinated* by becomes *fastened* to me.
- If you can't be excited about something, you can't make it happen.
- Enthusiasm is contagious, too. When you get excited, other people will catch it.
- If you're not growing, you're not going anywhere.
- Enthusiasm can work for you or against you; it depends on what you're enthusiastic *about.*
- If you're not excited, who will be?
- When you start with what you have, you realize that you never have just a little.

THE WORD: "Delight thyself also in the Lord; and he shall give thee the desires of the heart."—PSALMS 37:4

REVEREND RUN: "Enthusiasm is all about starting with what you have.... Enthusiasm will color the whole way you see the world.... It's what you need to get wherever you want to go. It's the feeling that makes you push forward when other people are giving up."

RUN'S HOUSE RULE

EXERCISE

Think back to one activity that you really enjoyed as a kid. If you can, today do it just for fun. If not, try developing some new hobby that you've perhaps thought about but never gotten around to trying.

11

LOVE AND BE LOVED

But the wisdom that is from above is first pure, then peace-able, gentle, and easy to be intreated, full of mercy and good fruits, without partiality, and without hypocrisy.
—James 3:17

WHEN EVERYTHING is going your way, of course everybody wants to be down with you. All the fakers. All the people who just want to get some kind of free ride. If you ever saw the VH1 *Behind the Music* episode with MC Hammer, you know what I'm talking about. He said at his height he had an entourage of three hundred people with him. Three hundred people! All traveling everywhere he went, staying in every hotel, and going to every show! He thought some of those people were his friends. He even had grown up with some of them. But after everything ground to a halt for him, do you know how many people were still there standing with him out of those three hundred people? *One.* That's right, one. His wife was the only person who stood by him. And he's lucky that he even had her. Some people don't have a single person who's real in their lives. I'm blessed because I have a lot of people in my corner: my father, my brothers, my wife and children, my band (Dee and Jay), and all of my fans.

Love is the most important thing in the world. If you didn't get love when you were little, it's hard to get over it. Everything that happens to your mom when she's pregnant with you is passed on to you. Medical studies have been done to show the effects of a mother's emotional well-being during pregnancy on the unborn child. Everything from what the mother eats to the types of music she listens to affects the baby. All in all, the womb is a nurturing environment that shelters us with warmth and love. That's the base—love. Once a child is born things can change radically. For example, I heard that in one country orphaned children are put in one big room in cribs that look more like cages. While they're fed, they aren't picked up, held, or even talked to, much less told that they are loved. They stay in these cribs all day long every day until one day maybe they are lucky enough to be adopted. At the age of three or four, they can't walk, they can't talk, and they're terrified of being picked up or being taken outside. And it can take them years with specialists just to be able to do those simple things. Their development is hurt because in their early years they were not given what had sustained them in the womb: love.

People don't understand love. They don't understand how Dee and Jay and I can still be down with one another after all these years. So many groups have broken up. So many friends have fallen out. So many people have said, "Screw this group; I'm doing my own thing." How have we always stayed together, even when the music wasn't getting any love? The answer is simple: we love one another. This is one of the reasons that our success didn't cost us our friendship. We were really best friends long before there was ever even any real thought of a hip-hop music career, much less Run-D.M.C.

There's no such thing as knowing God all by yourself. And having people in your life who will be with you when the chips are down is the most important thing. So how do you create relationships like that? And how do you know if the people around you are for real?

People don't understand how I could be so in love with Justine that I call her and talk to her for hours when I'm on tour in Japan and it costs me a fortune every minute just to use the phone. They don't understand how love also lets us talk to each other without even speaking.

If you want to bring love into your life, the first thing you have to do is stop expecting the worst of people. We usually suspect the worst in people. Stop; look; listen. See what's really happening. Does it really matter what happened twenty minutes ago? Are you holding onto stuff? Are you expecting the worst out of people? Do you think: *The girl next door is trying to get my man? The person in the next cubicle is trying to get my job? The guy in the subway is going to rob me?* If so, don't be surprised when what you're afraid of happens. The person wasn't even looking at you with that in mind, but you brought it into manifestation. You need to change that thought pattern. You have to see the good in everybody. You have to focus on the good part and ignore the rest. Everybody is put in your life for a reason. If somebody curses me out, it's a test for me and not something for me to react to and get bent out of shape about.

GO WHERE YOU'RE CELEBRATED, NOT TOLERATED

People who love you build you up, not tear you down. Sometimes you have to get out of your old environment if you want to create a new one. Sometimes you have to go where you're celebrated, not tolerated. Dee and his friends celebrated me. But in my neighborhood I was surrounded by dream killers.

Growing up on my block, I believe I got too familiar with people and they got too familiar with my talents. But when I went up around Dee's neighborhood, they would all give me respect and I would feel welcomed. At home, I felt like I wanted to *fly*, but I wasn't really able to. I always felt like there were a lot of dream killers around me when I was nine, ten, eleven, and twelve. I was trying to express myself and I knew I was good, but I felt like people wouldn't give me a chance.

Dee and I met in elementary school. I lived on 205th Street, and Dee lived on 197th Street. One day I went to his house with a bunch of other guys to play basketball. Dee and I had kind of known each other since the first grade, but it was when we began playing basketball together that we really started to get down with each other. I would walk all the way to Dee's neighborhood by myself, and I was still a kid.

Where Dee lived wasn't the heart of Hollis, Queens, with all the murders and robberies, but it was still busy down at Dee's end of Hollis. It's amazing to me when I think back—our daily routine basically consisted of smoking weed, getting high, listening to music, and "having fun," whatever that meant. When I came around, I would just be hilarious.

It was totally the opposite of the way I was persecuted in my own neighborhood. When I went around Dee's neighborhood, on 197th Street, I would be the life of the party and the center of attention. I would impersonate people—Bill Cosby or whomever. I would just talk all day. It was like an endless flow. I would just make people laugh talking about whatever was going on at the moment.

Dee and I really got to be good friends when we were playing basketball with the Police Athletic League (PAL). That was how I made my break from the block. That's how I got away from the people I felt didn't let me grow. I was really good at basketball back then, and in contrast to the harassment I received in my own neighborhood, basketball gave me a little chance to shine. I always felt like I could do more in life. I knew I was good in sneakers and I knew I was funny, but I couldn't get myself to a place of total confidence in what I knew I could do.

The love we developed back then is why Dee and I, and later Jay, were able to become so tight—and remain that way to this day. That's why we were so tight onstage and so loved and adored by millions and created a whole generation of music and fashion — because all three of us had a ton of respect for one another.

Looking back, I see that going where I was celebrated, not just tolerated, was the key to my total liberation. Getting away from the close-minded people on my block helped me to become confident in everything I did. I just formed a new perspective on who I was and what I could do. That's why you need to be around people who are not dream killers but dream builders.

Dee, Jay, and I have never had an argument. We don't argue. The respect level is so high it's crazy. For people to understand how to love, they have to understand: *If you want to have respect, you have to give respect. If you want love, you have to give it.*

People always ask Dee how he could put up with me all these years. People would talk behind my back and say to Dee, "He's mean. He's bugging. Why do you like him? Why are you so nice to him? Tell me how you do it?" But Dee didn't listen and loved me just the same.

Now I'm a new person and I heard Dee telling someone the other day about the new me: "Now he won't degrade you or belittle you. Before he was like, 'I'll fire you.' Now if the workers are doing something that's messing up the whole group he doesn't take it personally. When he fights, he's fighting for me and Jay, just like before he used to just fight for Run. Now it's not like he's saying, 'I'm the leader of the group,' but 'I gotta watch out for Jay and Dee.' "

Dee says now I care about people's feelings — not just myself. But even when I wasn't that way, Dee understood me and accepted me as I was, and that's why we were able to grow spiritually together. Today Dee is a deacon in the same church that I belong to.

The electricity between us was and is always so big. Ours is a tremendous relationship that ended up with us reading each other's thoughts. To this day onstage we know how to walk together without any rehearsal; we know how to gel together without knowing — it's almost like a marriage. And just like a marriage, what God has put together let no man put asunder. Me and Dee and Jay always knew that we were joined together for destiny's purpose. It's not about money; it's not about music. It's about love, respect, and living for a divine purpose.

BE ON THE SAME TEAM

Speaking of marriage, mine is perhaps the biggest blessing in my life. My wife, Justine, is truly on my team as I am on hers. And just like I met Dee when I was a kid, I met Justine when I was just a teenager. We fell out of contact for more than twelve years—and during that time, as you know, I had my ups and downs. But God blessed us with each other when we were both ready.

It's a wild story, how we met. One day, I think in 1979 or so, I was performing at the Roosevelt Skating Rink on Long Island. Everybody had come to see the headliner, Kurtis Blow. I was just a kid who performed a little number here or there as the Son of Kurtis Blow. Kurtis Blow's hot record back then was "The Breaks." Justine and her girls came to the show, all excited to come to the little concert. They thought they were rappers, too. I wasn't known at all; I just came out at the end of the show. Everybody wanted to meet Kurtis Blow, but Justine had her eye on me. She wrote this little letter and gave it to a cook at the rink and told him, "Give this to the guy who's with Kurtis Blow, *not* to Kurtis Blow." So this little note said that she wanted to meet me. We met and talked for a few minutes, and she gave me a piece of paper with her phone number on it, and two days later I called her.

I lived in Queens and she lived on Long Island. That was like a world apart to us back then, like her being on the back side of the moon, so we couldn't really see each other much. I say during our puppy-love "boyfriend-girlfriend" relationship we probably saw each other a total of three or four times. But we talked on the phone all the time. In fact, you could say we fell in love over the phone. I wrote letters to her constantly. One thing about me is that I'm really a sweet, affectionate guy, believe it or not. It wasn't what she expected, because I was supposed to be this hard-core guy.

I called her Sugarcane (which was her nickname back then). One of the few times we actually saw each other, I remember, was when we went to the movies on Jamaica Avenue. Then we just lost touch with each other. She was a little younger than me and couldn't see me much. She didn't know anyone in Queens. And it just faded away.

Twelve years passed.

I was on her mind, but she didn't know what had happened to me. I thought about her a lot and wondered where she was and what she was doing, but I didn't even have a way to contact her. She knew me as Joe. She had a picture of me, and one day this guy saw it and said to her, "You know who that is? That's Run from Run-D.M.C." Before, she never put the two together. Years later her sister happened to run into one of my cousins who was bragging, "My cousin is Run." And Justine's sister said, "What? My sister used to go with him." That's how we reconnected. My cousin came back and told me what had happened to Justine.

The first time Justine and I talked after all those years it was literally like no time had passed. We were both teenagers again. She thought I would be like, "Yo, whassup? How ya doin'?" all into the streets and so-called hip-hop life, but I wasn't. I just called her and said, "Hi." She says that's what got her right then — that shy part of me. She told me later that when I said, "Hi," she just felt like she had to take care of me.

Sometimes I say, "Why did we break up? We could have been together all along." And she says maybe God knew she couldn't deal with me as the person I was over all those years we were out of contact with each other. That's possible. I do think God knew we weren't ready. But really you never know the reason that something did or didn't happen.

What I do know is that our spiritual growth is something that has happened together. We did it together. She grew up in a loving home but wasn't someone who went to church every Sunday. But something I was doing in my own spiritual growth caught on inside her and she grabbed it and loved every moment of it.

It's a part of the secret of the success of our marriage. We feel God in everything we do, even in disagreements. She says before she met me she was the jealous type. We want a relationship that's on a level that most people can't even understand. That's why when we decided we were going to get together we didn't make love until we got married. We felt if we did, God was not going to let us get married. So it's fear of Him that keeps us in line. We wanted to prove to Him that we were listening to Him.

You know how relationships can be when they first start? People go out a lot together and have romantic dinners. Those things mean a lot to people. But they do them in the beginning and then stop. We always said we didn't want that to happen to our marriage. We don't want it to stop, because it doesn't have to. Whatever you did in the beginning you can do again. Sometimes I take her and the kids to Trump International Hotel & Towers or whatever so we all can get a break. And sometimes I just take her so we can spend quality time together. We try to excite each other and surprise each other. I'm about what makes Justine happy, and she's about what makes me happy. The important thing is that it's not just all about me and it's not all about her. We're linked together.

Whether it's in a romantic relationship, a business relationship, or a family relationship, you've got to have love and respect, and you've got to work together. If there's no trust, there's nothing. Sometimes you're better off without someone in your life if that person is going to hold you back from your blessings.

FINDING THE LOVE IN YOUR LIFE

Sometimes love means letting go of one thought to make room for another. Love means you can't hold onto stuff that doesn't matter. Let's say Justine and I have a minor disagreement because the craziest stuff just happened. We say things we don't mean. At the end we see that we're not coming to any conclusions. We have to be able to say, "None of that matters." We have to be able to say, "Let's not look back but forward and start all over again fresh." But if we're not careful, we will have created more problems than existed in the first place.

When you hold onto bitterness and grudges, you block your blessings. It could be your parents, brothers and sisters, children, friends, or whoever. If you don't let things go, you hold back your blessings, whether you know it or not. The secret to love is letting unimportant things go so that you can focus on the important things. Just let it go, and let your love flow.

No. 11

Love Is Giving

God is love. God loved the world so He gave His only begotten Son. God is all about giving. So, when God gave us Jesus that was His seed of giving. Now, look at the followers of the Christian faith because of that seed He gave of Jesus. Remember this: God is love.

It is in that giving that we know the seeds of love that we sow are just giving a little piece of the God that is inside us. When you look at your children and they look like you, favor your likeness, know that we were made in God's image and likeness and the bible says: "Ye are Gods, Cats of cats, God makes Gods."

It's Like This . . .
- There's no such thing as knowing God all by yourself.
- It's important to know who will be with you when the chips are down.
- If you want to bring love into your life, the first thing you have to do is stop expecting the worst of people.
- Go where you're celebrated, not tolerated.
- If you want to have respect, you have to give respect. If you want love, you have to give it.
- Life is a team sport. Create a team if you want to win.

THE WORD: ". . . For unto whomsoever much is given, of him shall be much required: and to whom men have committed much, of him they will ask the more."—LUKE 12:48

REVEREND RUN: "People who love you build you up, not tear you down. Sometimes you have to get out of your old environment if you want to create a new one. . . . Looking back, I see that going where I was celebrated, not just tolerated, was the key to my total liberation. Getting away from the close-minded people on my block helped me to become confident in everything I did. I just formed a new perspective on who I was and what I could do. That's why you need to be around people who are not dream killers but dream builders."

12

CREATE A WEALTH MENTALITY

"And be not conformed to this world: but be ye transformed by the renewing of your mind, that ye may prove what is that, and acceptable, and perfect, will of God."
—Romans 12:2

EARLIER WE TALKED about how the rich take chances, how people with a wealth mentality aren't afraid to go out on a limb. Now I'm going to add a little footnote on that. It's not just that the rich take chances. It's that people with a wealth mentality don't see things as potential failures but as successes just waiting to happen. When they look at a project, a proposal, or an idea, they don't sit there and say, "Boy, this is risky." They see all the good things about it and all the ways it's bound to succeed. Some wealthy people keep other people around them just to help them see any potential downside to new projects, because they always get caught up in seeing the upside. People who have a wealth mentality just don't see the same risks in things as other people do.

People with a poverty consciousness will always sit on the sidelines and watch a person with a wealth mentality go and accomplish some great feat and bend over and say, "Ooh, you could have hurt yourself doing that!" Some people just want to pick up the leaves off the ground, but other people have the faith to go up and get the grapes. Get off the sidelines and get into the game.

If you desire wealth, refrain from thinking about money in terms of how much you don't have. If you're unemployed and looking for work, you should wake up every morning brimming with enthusiasm, confident that you will get a job. You should laugh at the idea of not having a paycheck. There's always somebody out there, someone very close to you perhaps, sitting behind his desk thinking to himself, *I need some help!*

Be confident that there is always somebody out there looking for what you have to offer, no matter what your area of expertise. The key to landing a gig is knowing without a doubt that standing in the unemployment line isn't for you. Achieving in life is all about always having a positive, uplifting attitude.

The Bible says: To him that have, more is given and to him that have not, even the little bit that he has will be taken away from him. It's part of a story where three men are each given a number of talents (gold coins). The first man gets three, the second man gets two, and the third man receives one. After a period of time had passed, the wealthy man who had given the three men the talents returned to check up on the men. The first man had turned his three talents into six. The second had turned his two talents into three. But the third man, who had gotten only one talent in the first place, still had only one. It turned out that he had been so full of feelings of lack that he had buried his one talent in the ground! The wealthy man took the one talent from the man who had buried it and gave it to the man who had started out with three talents. If you don't know how to use what you have, God is going to take it away from you.

The key to being ready to accept blessings is to sift through and let go of feelings of lack. Everything in this universe has to move and circulate. If blood stops flowing through your veins then you'll die. That's why they call money currency. It flows. When you hoard it things get messed up. Don't believe me? Try holding your breath for a long time. Do it right now. It's impossible to do. You'll pass out. In order to get a new breath you must first give up one. If you hoard your money and don't let it flow, you become financially dead. That doesn't mean that you don't save. It just means that you let go of the feeling that says you're not going to be provided for, so you have to bury your blessings.

It's no coincidence that the currency was called talents. Our talents are our abilities and they are our wealth. In this story, the one talent that the third man received was taken back from him by the lender and given to the first man, who he knew would put it to good use and make it grow. What we don't use and nurture we lose, whether it's our abilities, friendships, or money. If you don't own something in your mind, even if you receive it physically, it will be taken away from you.

If everybody in the world were given a million dollars in cash today, I guarantee you in a very short amount of time 95 percent of the people who were poor before they got the million dollars would be poor again. Water seeks its own level. And you can't have physically more than you have mentally.

The world truly is this way. I'll give you an example. If you have in your consciousness that you are the greatest at doing a particular thing and even if nobody but you knows that you are the greatest, in time you will see you are becoming what you are holding in your mind.

Donald Trump is a good example of a wealth mentality. As the story goes, a few years ago he lost a great deal of money with the depressed real estate market. He was a laughingstock. He went out, played golf, and didn't worry. He and his wife, Ivanna, were walking down a block, and he pointed to a bum sitting on a curb and said, "That guy right there has more money than me."

His wife asked, "How?"

"Because I'm one hundred and fifty million dollars in the hole. He has no debt, no problems. He has more than me at this point." That's how broke Trump was.

But Trump already had a wealth consciousness. He knew how to go out and buy a building with a penny. He knew in his heart he was a multibillionaire. He let himself be calm and in the game until the real estate market turned around and put him back into the black. Back into billionaire status.

A guy across the street from me back in the day had a poverty consciousness. One day he hit the Lotto. Six months later he was broke. Although he did have a million, it meant nothing to him.

Trump lost it all and gained it back in a few years. My neighbor got it, lost it all, and never regained it. He's homeless and broke now, in worse shape than before. All this goes to show that money is not a physical thing. It comes to you as an effect. There's a cause and effect. The effect is the cash. You have it because you believe you have it . . . and deserve it.

The guy who hit the Lotto didn't have confidence in being a millionaire and didn't believe he deserved it and squandered the money. Again, water sought its own level and flowed right there. The money found its level in him. And he didn't deserve any of it, and it all washed away. Mind seeks its own level. He didn't have the right consciousness. Now when I see a tight financial situation, I go further into it to tell my self-consciousness that lack is not a reality. Instead of holding back, I go forward, which people tell me is not very smart; no one can understand why I am successful.

Being ready for wealth is a big part of having your buckets ready. You have to be prepared for wealth. The very rich with their millions and billions often give their children a few pennies and say, "Go make it yourself!" And when the wise do give, they rarely give it immediately, without the proper training, because they realize their children may squander it. That's the key to life, having the right consciousness.

Some people blame their lot in life on everything but themselves. We like to have something to blame so we can say, "I'm not succeeding

141

and it's because of him or her." Instead of finding something to blame, you have to look inside yourself. We're all given our own unique gifts. Most people die with their gifts still locked away inside them, without succeeding with them. To find your wealth look at where your talents are.

THE WEALTHY DON'T FAIL

One thing that people with a wealth mentality have in common is that they don't fail. That doesn't mean that they don't start companies that go out of business or make products that nobody buys. It means that they don't give up. They don't look at one little so-called failure as meaning their whole life was a failure. Sure, Run-D.M.C. made an album that did terrible. We made a movie that was a horrible flop. Did we just say, "Forget it all," and throw in the towel? No! I thought about it when I was depressed, but something inside me just wouldn't let me do it. And the group, we just kept plugging away. Failure is something that is reserved for people who don't understand the way the world really works and the power of their own minds.

What happens to the guy who doesn't plan? He's the one who fails. And what is failure? Failure is only giving up. You never fail until you give up completely. Failure is a story that can only be told in the end, when everything can be added up to see who never quit on life.

I believe that sometimes, when one generation dies leaving dreams unfulfilled, that dream passes on to the children of the next generation. Does God require that of us? Maybe He does. Did I become the Reverend Run in order to fulfill a dream that started four generations ago? I don't know. I try to empty myself out so that my son Joey Jr. and my other children don't have to go forth and live my dreams. We cannot say now what God has in store for them or any other people. Whether we have to live our parents' dreams or not, we are all put here for a reason and sometimes more than one reason—and failure doesn't fit into the picture.

I have to be a rapper and a reverend and now an author! Maybe something else at some point in the future, who knows? What I do know is that failure only comes when you finally give up. Who knows what older people have in store for them? Look at George Foreman, at fifty knocking people out and looking great. Someone probably told him he was too old to be a champion boxer. But obviously he didn't listen. He just knew that he was the kind of person who was destined for success. No one knows the capacity of man, and we might never know. But we are always getting better.

Somebody is going to do something very amazing in the next couple of years that we're going to be bugging about. Maybe it will be a new invention. Maybe it will be a new type of music. I don't know what it will be, but I do know for sure that things like this will happen. Life is going to be getting more and more exciting as we make more discoveries and get better and better at living.

God constantly brings these brilliant people on this earth. Doctor J was the best thing ever until Michael Jordan came along. Who would have thought sometime back they would write that Puffy was one of the best rappers around—that he'd be selling millions of records? Ten years ago you might have put your money on L. L. or somebody who at least we knew as a rapper. Whoever. But how many of us would have put money on the fact that Puffy would be up to whatever he's going to sell, maybe 8 million albums, next year? The bottom line is we don't know much. *We don't even know the limits of our own potential.* According to medical researchers, the average person uses something like less than 15 percent of his brainpower. Imagine if you just used 20 percent. You'd be miles ahead of everybody else! Why accept failure or limitations? I'll let you in on another secret: You are one of the brilliant people God has brought to the earth, whether you know it or not. You have the potential to be the best in the world at something. You have the potential to be successful in a field that doesn't even exist yet. You don't know what's coming down the pike, and that's why you have to expect the unexpected. And if you want to, you can even decide to take charge of your mind and create that next thing that's going to come down that pike.

RUN'S HOUSE RULE

No. 12

You Deserve It All

I want it all and why not? There is nothing wrong with dreaming big. There is nothing wrong with wanting a big house, a fancy car, and a nice family. But you have to work for it. You have to work very hard to keep it. And you have to dream very big to achieve it. You do deserve it all.

It's Like This . . .
- Money is not a physical thing.
- Have money, but don't let money have you.
- If you desire wealth, stop thinking about money in terms of how much you *don't* have.
- If you don't know how to use what you have, God is going to take it away from you.
- If you hoard your money and don't let it flow, you become financially dead.
- If you don't own something in your mind, even if you receive it physically it will be taken away from you.
- You never fail until you give up completely.
- So never give up!

THE WORD: "What shall we then say to these things?"—ROMANS 8:31

REVEREND RUN: "Be confident that there is always somebody out there looking for what you have to offer, no matter what you have to offer, no matter what your area of expertise is. The key to landing a gig is knowing without a doubt that standing in the unemployment line isn't for you. Achieving in life is all about always having a positive, uplifting attitude."

13

MY CROWN IS ROYAL: BE A PIONEER

For by grace are ye saved through faith; and that not of yourselves: it is the gift of God: not of works, lest any man should boast.

—Ephesians 2:8-9

MY CROWN IS ROYAL! Let me tell you about Run right now, today. I went to God. I got myself together, and now I'm a rich young ruler, with a Bible under his arm. My life story is not, "I was rich, hated being rich, and now I'm saved and poor." Today I'm richer than ever. I'm very materialistic on the one hand, but it's not the same as it was back then. I've got control over it. There's a real power in Reverend Run not being broke and telling you to come get down with God now. There's a real power in Run being rich. With the principles I've tried to share with you in this book, I hope to help you understand how to have money without letting money have you.

My gift, my diamond, that I was seeking was the gift that had always been with me—my tongue. Remember, ever since I was a little kid, my mouth was running. But when I rewrote the script of my life, I learned how to make my power the most effective it could be: I learned to be a minister. I learned that I could share what had helped me to turn my life around with other people.

How many rappers have become reverends? Not many, that's for sure. None other than me that I know of. I don't say this to brag; I say this so that you'll understand I'm just blazing a new trail now. When I first became a reverend it wasn't cool at all. Now you have people like Kirk Franklin blowing up the charts making gospel albums and everybody says, "Wow, maybe there's something to this." But either way, I've had to bear the weight of being a pioneer. And the responsibility that comes with it.

Some people think I'm some kind of mad genius, but I'm the most ridiculous human being on the earth to Russell, my father, and lots of other people. Russell once said, "You're a fool. You become this reverend. Your career is not doing that well and you go and buy this million-dollar house. And I hear that you've got another Mercedes and your American Express bill this month is twenty-two thousand dollars." He said it just didn't make any sense for me to be living like I was. To him, I looked like the most far gone, ridiculous human being on the earth because I lived by faith. My father thought I was crazy, too.

In the beginning that's what everybody thought. My father said, "Now you sound like that Reverend Ike." Russell's thing was, "What does God have to do with money and prosperity?" My response was, "What does God have to do with *poverty* and *ill health*? I'm here for prosperity, I'm here for health, and I'm here for joy and happiness." Then people turned to me and said, "Joey, as a minister you should not be concerned with materialism." I looked them in the face and said, "How am I ever gonna get the attention of the people who ever loved Run? Become a minister and say, 'I'm broke. I'm a reverend. Fans of old, follow me now'? And I jump into a Pinto and pull off?" Nobody would follow me. I had to be different and let people know that it's your birthright to be healthy, happy, successful, and yes, prosperous — and that being those things doesn't mean you can't be down with God.

If I tried to do something that somebody else was doing I wouldn't be successful. I had to go within myself and say, *God is within me. What do You want me to do, God?* When I asked that question, He gave me the answer. You have to go within yourself and ask the same question. You can't wait for God to make things happen. That's the story of my life. I am a miracle worker. This is how I walk. People see me as that. I heard somebody at my church say, "Minister Simmons creates miracles daily." That's what I do. I create my environment with my mind. Whether you know it or not . . . we all do.

When Jesus was on earth, he understood that he could heal people. The better people understand what their power is, the more they will be able to walk in their divinity, and that's where perception comes in. *Whatever you believe you can do, you can do.* You cannot go past the capacity of what you believe you can do. The further we get off into what we believe we can do the more we will accomplish. That's how inventions come into fruition.

The point is that innovators get laughed at. "I can fly." "I'm going to walk on the moon." Imagine how that would sound if you were hearing it for the first time, before flight and rocket boosters? There will always be naysayers. People always laugh at pioneers, because what they are doing is something that has never been down before. I was a pioneer along with Dee and Jay when we came out with this all-new dress code for rap back in 1983. Now, I am breaking down new barriers for the world of hip-hop and giving honor and grace to God for bringing me back by simply being the Reverend Run. I am breaking down new barriers by being a rap artist who has written a book that talks about helping and improving yourself instead of just talking about my past.

When it was time for me to grow, it was just time for me to grow. I always took whatever I did to the extreme because I was always a person who felt destined for success. I believe that I had to go and get with God, and that's why I'm the Reverend Run. I attribute my comeback and all the good things happening now, like this book, to my relationship with and faith in God. I had to come through all those bad times, losing my first wife and the hell I went through, to be able to plant new seeds and learn the right way to live. It was all a blessing.

Today I'm more successful than ever. First of all, Run-D.M.C. is the Rolling Stones of hip-hop. We perform about three hundred shows a year all around the world! Recently a young man named Jason Nevins made a remix of our classic song "It's Like That," which inspired the title of this book. The techno remix soared to number one throughout Europe. All of a sudden I was back on top of my music. But what's even more important to me is that I now have a newfound appreciation for life and my place in the world. Now I have the Mercedes, the Rolls-Royce, the customized limo, the diamond Rolex, but this time it's different. Those things don't control me. I control them and I have them in the proper perspective. I always put first things first.

"If It Sounds Crazy, Count Me In"

I once heard a preacher say, "If it sounds crazy, count me in." I like to live by that motto. If it looks sane, I don't want to be around it. Most of the things I do that create the miracle seem crazy, not the way to go.

The best things in life are always simple. Music producer Jermaine Dupri talks about the way he makes his hits from *simple* things. You have some of the greatest musicians in the world right now who can play the bass guitar better than anything you have heard, then Jermaine Dupri comes along and makes some of the biggest hits that the world has ever seen. In one of his hit records the lyrics say: *"Mac daddy make it jump, jump"*—the simplest idea in the world and it sells millions. You have to be able to take the simple thing.

God has taken the foolish things of this world to confound the wise. Was that me? Who would have thought the messiah would be born in

Nazareth, a small, poor town, while everybody was looking everywhere else for the child of God? Jesus was born and the wise men followed the star. They found the little baby, not in the finest hospital, but in a manger next to the sheep, because there was no room at the inn. I'm telling you, the answer could be right under your nose. If Jesus were to come today, he wouldn't be in the finest kingdom or having the finest upbringing and we would probably have to go to the heart of a place in Harlem to find him. It's the small things. It's the things that nobody expects to work. The things you think are foolish. It might seem to you that things aren't going right financially, but what you need to do is not give this an audience.

Don't think in terms of things being upside down, but think they're right side up. In other words, the advice that I give to people and the method that works for me every time is if you fall off your horse, jump up and get right back on. Don't let go.

If things aren't going your way, brush your teeth, put on your clothes, get that haircut, and move forth as if everything is all right. The millionaire is the person conscious of believing, *I am wealthy*, regardless of physical appearances. You cannot feed into the illusion that things are wrong, because the second you do that your life gets crazy. And it will get worse because now you're giving it attention and anything you give attention to will continue to perform.

You cannot give an audience to poverty, you cannot give an audience to lack, and you cannot give an audience to ill health. When you do not give them an audience, those same conditions will evaporate like water on a sunny day. They have to. They have no audience. There's nobody caring about them. So since there is nobody caring, they won't tap-dance any longer. Don't give things your power. You're more powerful than sickness. You're more powerful than poverty. You're more powerful than disease. For Justine and me, when things got to be lacking we would take our last couple of hundred dollars and instead of buying groceries, dress the kids in their best clothes and take them to the finest restaurant, because we weren't scared that we were never going to have money again. We didn't pay the lack any attention. We found that the dinner would clear our heads and allow us to actually think about positive solutions. And invariably, the next day a check or a job would come up. The more you give lack attention, the worse off you'll be in life. These principles I'm kicking to you are real. I didn't make them up. You can read the stories of successful people or people who pioneered one thing or another and you will see that they put these principles to work in their lives. Understanding these principles and putting them to work is how you make a change in your life. That type of living can open up doors for success.

It's a sad thing when you see a grown person stuck in one spot in life. I saw a guy the other day on the street, and he said to me, "Run, come on; give me seventy-five cents to throw down on this forty." He wanted me to put in half so that we could share a forty-ounce bottle of beer. I'm thinking to myself, *This is ridiculous. I'm a grown man watching my kids jump out of a Jaguar. I'm thirty-four years old and he wants to drink a beer with me. He was my friend years ago. That's what we used to do when we were fifteen or sixteen.* It is just sad to see that some people never grow. And that's the difference between somebody who is moving forward in life and somebody who's not.

Remember, the time comes when you must put away childish things. I believe that a lot of us have done childish things in our youth and some of us have put them away and some of us are still dealing with those things. My wife tells me about some places she used to go and how her little sister goes to parties now and still sees the same people from my wife's era. These people never grew up. They're still doing the same thing. But times change and you have to change. *When you don't grow, the world wipes you out.* The world waits for nobody to grow. The wind comes along and pulls up your roots and you die. You need to be strong. The strong survive. You can always see some of the people you knew back in the day who aren't achieving, aren't moving forth. That's just the way life is. That's peer pressure, but you can't succumb to peer pressure after a certain age.

Change is never an easy thing. That's why people get caught up. But I think you can always change if you're a survivor. It's one reason you picked up this book: You have a zest for life and really want to win. You can't do the same thing over and over and expect new results. That is definitely called insanity. If every day you eat three pieces of cheesecake, four cheeseburgers, and french fries, and drink Coke and you expect to one day lose weight, you're a fool. When you start doing something new, something new is going to happen to you. If you start running and you start eating right, you're going to lose weight. Change is not an easy thing.

The universe is a teacher. If you don't get it from a real teacher, the world kicks your butt. The universe wants you to move on. If you don't learn from the appointed teacher, the universe will teach you. Some people will just go on and on doing the same things and they'll just eventually fall off. But I think that those who really want to win will reach down and try to figure out what they have to do to survive. I don't care if you're black, white, Chinese, Mexican, or whatever. If you want to win, you go find a formula that helps you win.

When I first found the Lord, the ministry was a test. I had to give it long and hard thought and take different baby steps to see if it was for me. I had to give myself a chance to adjust. Change. Later I found out that it did work. So I found a life formula for me. That's the key. You have to find a life formula for you that works. You have to find something that bears fruit, or gets you positive results. Maybe what works for you is different from what works for me. But if you're dealing with something that's not bearing any fruit in your life, you are destined to fail sooner or later. Get rid of it. Change! You can do it!

When you find something in life that works, it won't always work for you the way you think it will. But it will show you signs that you're on the right path to what you want to achieve. In the midst of my being at Zoe was when my first wife left me. That's when my finances got worse. I think that the thing that makes me the happiest when I think of my success in becoming a minister is that I faced the challenge of holding onto the truth and the belief that things will work out. If you read the stories of great people, they all say the same thing: these people always held on when things got bleak. I love the challenge.

I had to counsel somebody recently about something that was going on in his life, and he was saying it seemed that nothing was working for him the way it was supposed to. My wife was feeling sorry for this person, and it seemed like whatever I said, this person just kept feeling down and dejected. God is so good that when I jumped into the tub a few hours later, I opened up a book where Bishop Jordan had underlined certain things. The things he underlined were exactly what the person I had been counseling needed to hear. After I sat in my tub to read it, I had to jump out and call this person and say, "You know what? The challenges you are going through now are nothing compared to the ones I went through. Hold on." I read all these great things from the book. I told him that he had to love challenge in the midst of waiting for triumph: "Life would love you to quit at eleven-fifty-nine when the breakthrough is at twelve. Most people do quit at eleven-fifty-nine and that's why you see only a few millionaires. The key to life is you must press on. *Even when it seems like it's not working, it is working.* Keep on keeping on! You can do it!"

People saw me getting out of my nice car and everybody looked to ridicule Reverend Run. But now they've seen my dedication and prosperity and believe I am the Reverend Run. Some have seen where it's coming from, so I re-create my task according to whatever I want to do. If I want to do something else tomorrow, I'll do it. This world is your stage, and you are the writer, the talent, the producer, and the director of your movie. The rapper, the star. When you get tired of playing a pauper, start playing a wealthy person, pick up the script, write it, and re-create yourself and go forward in your consciousness that says, Now

I am rich, and you play that over and over every day until it takes on a total reality. Until that inner conversation and your outer manifestation become one.

I regret certain things and that's what this book's about. I'm here to give you wisdom. They say wisdom comes with age. Well, I'm not really an elder, but in the world of hip-hop I am an elder, if you know what I mean. I have been doing this since I was twelve. I'm not that old, but I do know how not to trip over the mike cord. I know how to rock a crowd. And I know how to do a lot of things that I'll never mess up with. Other rappers tell me honestly, "Who else can I talk to but you, Run? Who else would know what I'm dealing with?" But I don't just share with rappers; I share with anybody who wants to hear about the path that I've walked thus far in my life. I preach to share the knowledge of the things I did that were correct and the things I did that were incorrect. You have to fall down in order to get up again. It's called a reality check. It's how you write the script that you want to read. The script is in your heart, and nobody can tell you what it is but you.

Remember, it's *your* play in *your* theater on *your* stage and with *your* script. So there is no excuse for not winning, especially when you control the action.

Whenever you're ready, start winning.

It's like that . . .

RUN'S HOUSE RULE

No. 13

Find Your Gifts

You are a star. Don't let anybody tell you otherwise. Everybody comes here with gifts. It takes time, but you will find your own. Peace and love, I'm out.

It's Like This . . .

- Whatever you believe you can do, you can do.
- God *wants* you to be prosperous.
- Innovators get laughed at because they are doing something that's never been done before.
- If it sounds crazy, count me in.
- The best things in life are always simple. God has created the foolish things of this world to confound the wise.
- When you don't grow, the world wipes you out.
- The universe wants you to move on. If you don't learn from the appointed teacher, the universe will teach you.
- The key to life is you must keep on. Even when it seems like it's not working, it's working.

THE WORD: "And we know that all things work together for good to them that love God, to them who are called according to his purpose."—ROMANS 8:28

REVEREND RUN: "My gift, my diamond, that I was seeking was the gift that had always been with me—was my tongue. Remember, ever since I was a little kid, my mouth was running. But when I rewrote the script of my life, I learned how to make my power the most efffective it could be: I learned to be a minister. I learned that I could share what had helped me to turn my life around with other people. . . . So, there is no excuse for not winning. Especially when you control the action."

Log in to RUN's HOUSE on the Web.

Now you can catch the latest news in the hip-hop community, read daily affirmations, and hear the latest sounds from the godfather of rap at *www.RevRun.com*. Once you are logged in, you will have access to winning free and exclusive merchandise, and be able to listen to live concert footage as well as chat directly with the Reverend Run.

Order Books

You can also order additional copies of this book and others like it by logging in to *www.stmartins.com*.

L-6